How To...

AUDIO ACCESS INCLUDED

Play Solo Jazz Piano

Chapters include: Chords & Voicings • Bass Lines Swing Tunes • Ballads • Improvisation

By John Valerio

To access audio visit:
www.halleonard.com/mylibrary

3592-7048-8780-7410

ISBN 978-1-4950-2788-8

7777 W. Bluemound Rd. P.O. Box 13819 Milwaukee, WI 53213

In Australia Contact:
Hal Leonard Australia Pty. Ltd.
4 Lentara Court
Cheltenham, Victoria, 3192 Australia
Email: ausadmin@halleonard.com.au

Visit Hal Leonard Online at
www.halleonard.com

CONTENTS

4	Introduction
6	Chapter 1 – Chords and Voicings
19	Chapter 2 – Voicing Tunes
27	Chapter 3 – Bass Lines
42	Chapter 4 – Harmonic Embellishment
49	Chapter 5 – Swing Tunes
66	Chapter 6 – Jazz Waltzes
74	Chapter 7 – Latin Jazz Tunes
84	Chapter 8 – Ballads
91	Chapter 9 – Improvisation
96	Appendix – Lead Sheets
102	About the Author

INTRODUCTION

Jazz first emerged in New Orleans in 1900. Its two main sources were ragtime and blues. While wind instrument players began adding blues inflections and ragtime-like rhythms to their music, pianists added blue notes and improvisation to theirs. From the beginning, jazz evolved simultaneously as a small band music and as a solo piano music. Solo jazz piano continued evolving from New Orleans to stride piano in the 1920s and to swing piano in the 1930s. The ragtime model served jazz piano through all these styles until bebop emerged in the 1940s.

Ragtime itself was modeled on march music; a strong sense of rhythm is characteristic of both. The left hand in ragtime keeps the pulse going, largely by alternating bass notes and chords. This oom-pah, oom-pah motion comes from the march and was an important component of early jazz piano; jazz pianists kept the left hand actively playing the beat – in both solo and group, performing along with the rest of the rhythm section. In the '40s, having the pianist keep the pulse in a group was thought redundant. Count Basie, during the Swing Era of the '30s, was the first band pianist to break free from the beat, comping chords randomly. In some ways, this was the beginning of the end of the era of the great solo pianists.

Most of the great solo jazz pianists were active during the first half of the 20th century. Jelly Roll Morton was the earliest of these and was one of the inventors of jazz. He was one of the first to combine elements of blues with ragtime. Morton took existing rags and improvised on them, thereby turning them into jazz, making each performance of a rag a unique personal statement. Jazz is primarily a performer's art; each new performance is essentially a new composition. The early New Orleans-style piano playing of Jelly Roll Morton gave way to stride piano in the '20s. The great stride players dazzled with their virtuosity. These include James P. Johnson, Fats Waller, and Willie "The Lion" Smith.

Stride turned into swing piano in the '30s, which streamlined stride and smoothed out its accents; the evenness of beats is characteristic of the swing style in general. The swing players used walking tenths in addition to the oom-pah in the left hand, which softened the sound. The facile single-note right-hand runs of the swing pianists often replaced the full-voiced right-hand chords of the stride players. While both Teddy Wilson and Art Tatum best represent the swing style, Art Tatum – who came from the stride period – took solo jazz piano to its highest level. Tatum brought ragtime-based jazz piano to its ultimate conclusion; the traditional art of solo jazz piano more or less died when he passed away in 1956.

Before bebop emerged in the 1940s, playing solo did not differ much from playing with a group: Pianists essentially kept the counting going in the left hand. But with the advent of left-hand comping, pianists relied on the rest of the rhythm section to make the beat audible. The solo pianist, however, has no such underpinning and must either supply the pulse himself or let go of it. Hence, solo piano and group piano have become two separate arts. Today, many pianists are equipped for playing with a group, but have little training in solo playing.

Though most prominent post-bop pianists have recorded solo from time to time, only Keith Jarrett has done so on a regular basis. The majority of Jarrett's solo performances, however, are spontaneous improvisations with no structural basis and are not founded on tunes per se. Thelonious Monk recorded several solo albums, but adapted stride piano techniques to his idiosyncratic pianism. Oscar Peterson's solo playing was deeply rooted in Art Tatum's conception. The father of modern jazz piano, Bill Evans, revolutionized the genre by developing the use of rootless left-hand voicings and clusters. Thus, the very sound of modern jazz piano engendered in these voicings infers the use of a bass player to underpin the harmonic function by supplying or inferring roots and root motion.

How, then, do we play modern solo jazz piano? "Very carefully," one might say. We must tread the fine lines among melody, harmony, and bass. Having only two hands presents some restrictions in the execution of these parameters, but none that are insurmountable. The trick is to give the illusion that all three are present. We can accomplish this by keeping the rhythmic impulse going through the composite rhythm among the parts. Of course, we can always play a continuous bass line in the left hand while playing melody and chords with the right hand. We can comp chords in the left hand while playing melody in the right hand and use a striding left hand as well. These approaches, however, place limitations on the subtle aspects of playing the piano and the coloristic options afforded by the composite technique. All these procedures are covered in this book, but the emphasis is on the composite one. Bill Evans effectively used this method in his solo performances; his solo playing differs from his trio playing in this regard. He compensates for the lack of a bassist by scaling down the lushness of his trio playing and in no way tries to be a one-man band. Melody, harmony, and bass are all there, but not necessarily all at the same time.

This book offers a step-by-step practical approach to learning and playing standard tunes by dissecting their component parts: melody, harmony, and bass. The parts are then reassembled in various ways. The first chapter reviews chords and assorted chord voicings. The remaining chapters describe ways of playing tunes in different styles that include swing, jazz waltz, Latin, and ballads. The last chapter offers some ideas on solo improvisation in these styles. This volume is not for beginners and assumes a certain familiarity with chords, voicings, technique, and styles. However, any pianist with a basic knowledge of these should be able to understand and apply the concepts presented here. Often, jazz pianists are called upon to play solo gigs. This publication attempts to ease the transition from group to solo jazz piano playing.

CHAPTER 1

CHORDS AND VOICINGS

The solo jazz pianist should have a vast repertoire of chords and chord voicings at his or her command. There are various ways a chord can be played and the improvising pianist makes instantaneous decisions in choosing a particular voicing. By having many options at our command, we can construct interesting and diverse arrangements in real time. We choose certain voicings depending on the style, feel, and tempo of the music, as well as textural, registral, and technical considerations. This chapter will outline some of the commonly used chords and voicings contemporary pianists use.

BASIC SEVENTH AND SIXTH CHORDS

For the most part, jazz uses the four-note seventh or sixth chord, not the triad, as a fundamental harmonic unit. The basic chord qualities are shown below for the root C. Learn and play them for all 12 root notes.

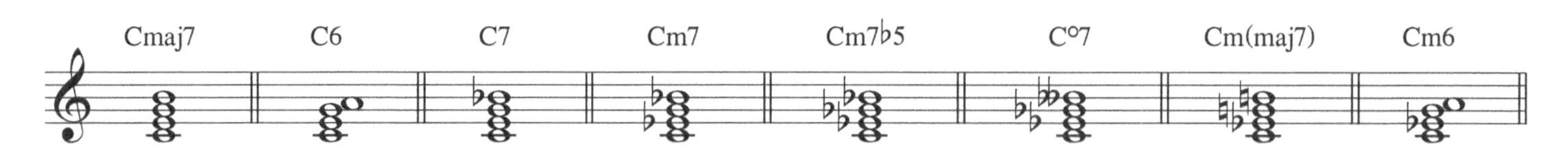

Likewise, you should be familiar with all inversions of these chords and play them in all 12 keys.

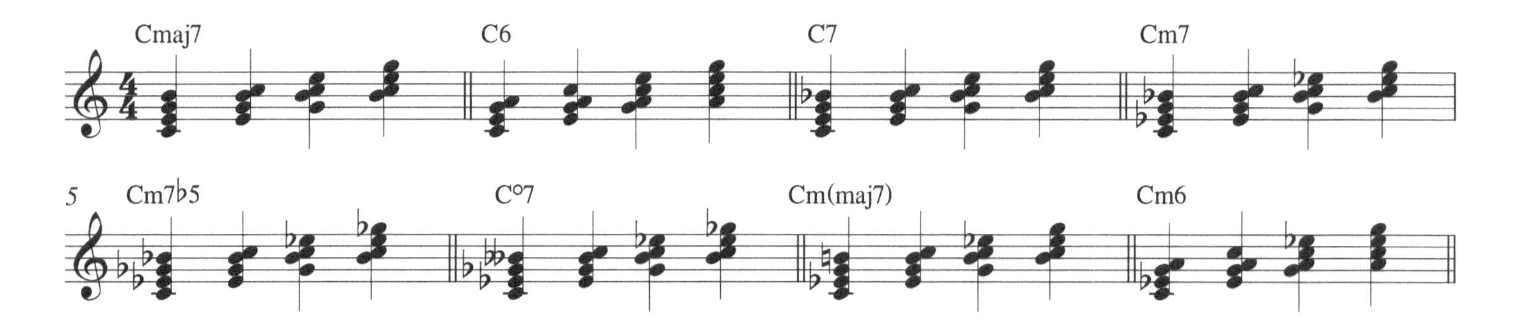

ALTERED DOMINANT SEVENTH CHORDS

Dominant seventh chords are sometimes modified as follows. These altered notes can sometimes be thought of as upper extensions: sus4 = 11; ♯5 = ♭13; ♭5 = ♯11.

VOICE LEADING AND GUIDE TONES

The connection of chords through smooth voice leading is a staple of all tonal music. Knowing chords is one thing, but knowing how to connect one to another is an art in itself. Jazz musicians usually do this by connecting guide tones, the third and seventh of a chord that smoothly connect to the seventh and third of a following chord whose root is a fifth lower. (This is the most common root movement.) Guide tones define the quality of a chord and thus are often more important than the root. Below is a ii-V-I progression in C major indicating the guide-tone voice leading within full chords, guide tones alone, and guide tones with roots.

Dm7 G7 Cmaj7 Dm7 G7 Cmaj7 Dm7 G7 Cmaj7

Guide tones work well with descending Circle of Fifths progressions that go beyond ii-V-I. This example is in A minor.

While group pianists often play guide tones alone while comping, solo pianists have the additional need to supply roots most of the time. Here, the previous progression is shown with roots.

Dm7 G7 Cmaj7 F Bm7♭5 E7 Am(maj7) A7

Hand stretches that expand the interval of a tenth can be problematic for some pianists – and not all stretches are equal in distance. Thus, some tenths are more playable than others. The roots and guide tones, however, do not have to be played at the same time, as demonstrated below.

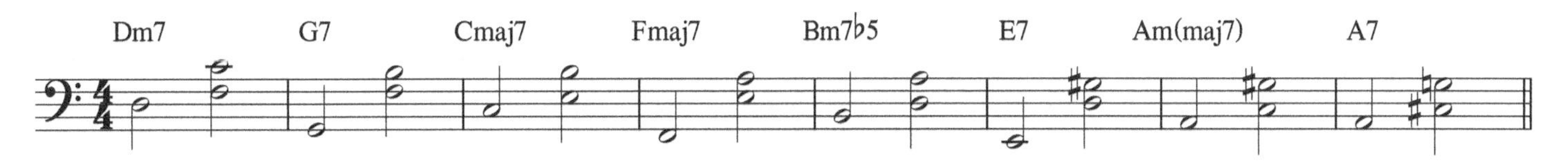

The third and seventh of the guide tones can change places and still progress smoothly. The following example shows how this works best, depending on the relative range of the chord voicings. This is the same progression as the previous examples transposed to E minor.

EXTENDED CHORDS

It is not practical to play ninth, eleventh, and thirteenth chords in one hand. Frequently, they are played either by leaving notes out or by spreading them between the hands. Here are the most common extended chords, shown in close position.

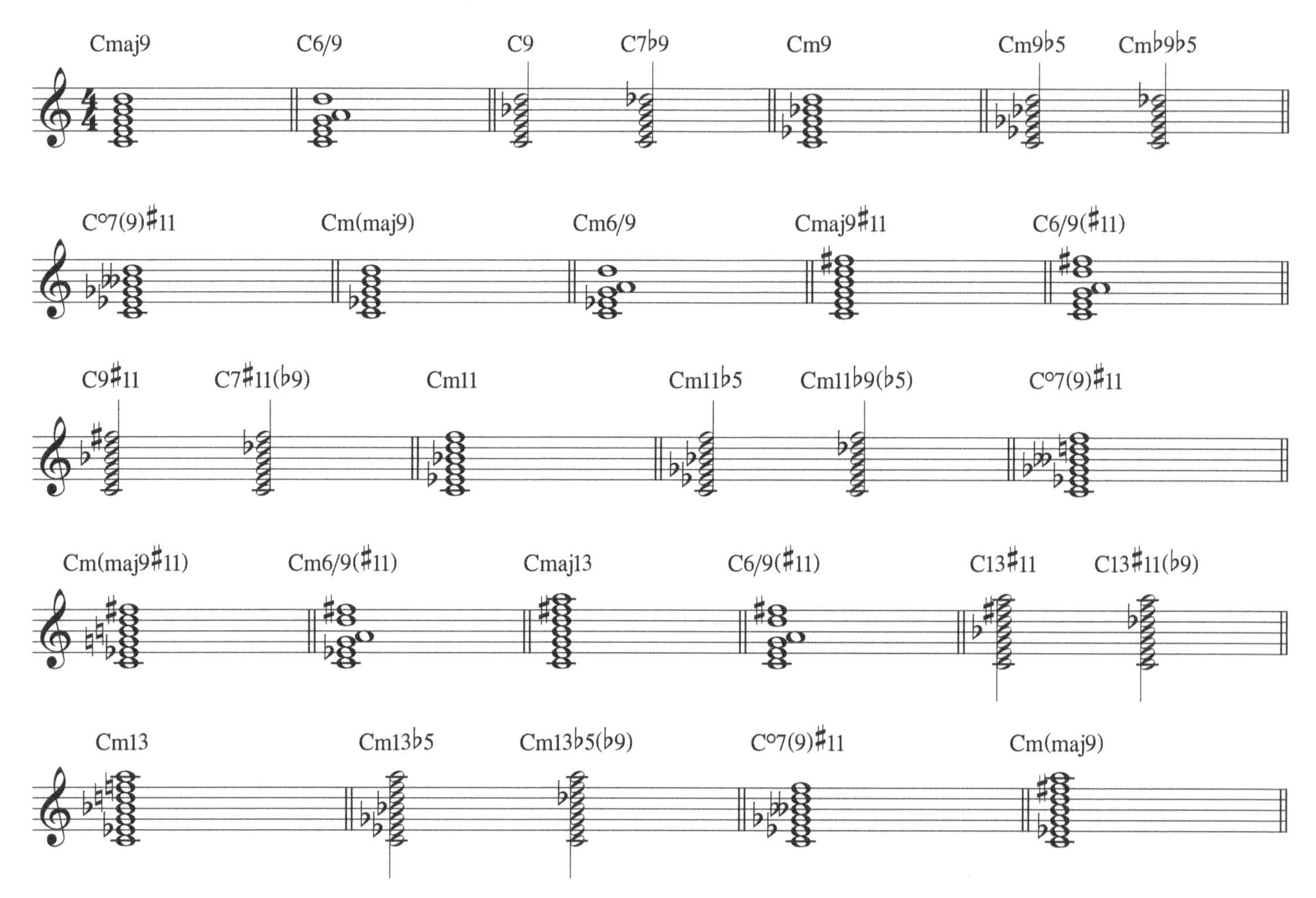

FOUR-NOTE OPEN VOICINGS FOR TWO HANDS

Standard open voicings for the basic chord qualities played in both hands are given below. The left-hand determines the voicing type. There are three types: 1-7, 1-3 or 1-10, and 1-5. The chord tones for each voicing are indicated for the first chord (Cmaj7) and are similar for those that follow. The right-hand notes are flipped only for the left-hand 1-5 type; the other right-hand voicings can be flipped also, but are not used as regularly because of the wider interval that results. Keep in mind that melody will be superimposed on top of these voicings. The examples here use 1-10 in the left hand as well as 1-3 since this tenth, C to E, is within reach of most pianists. Other tenths, such as B♭-D, often are not practical; therefore, a third rather than a tenth can be used. You can employ a third instead of a tenth for any voicing in this book.

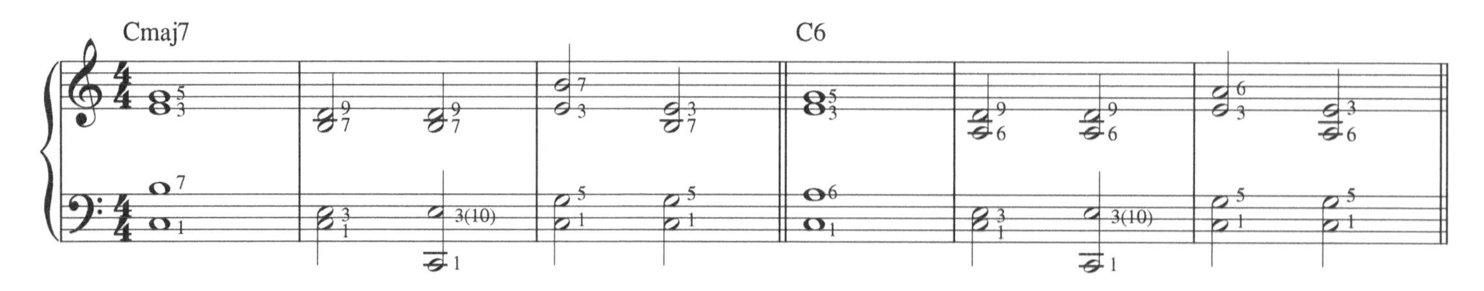

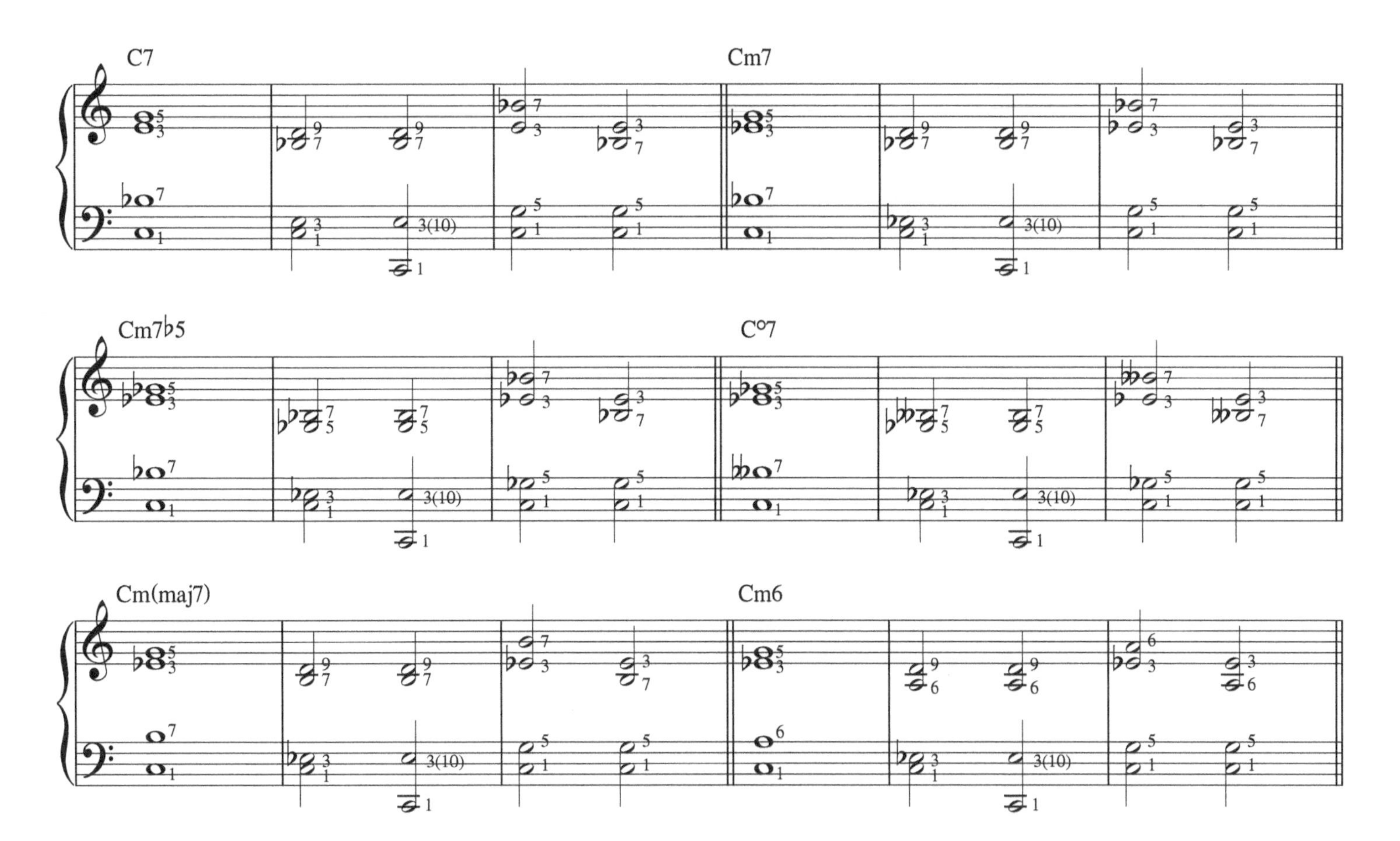

Four-note open voicings often are used in combinations. In descending Circle of Fifths progressions like ii–V–I, the 1-7 left-hand voicing frequently is followed by a 1-3(10) left-hand voicing and vice versa; this allows for smooth voice leading in the right hand and smooth guide tone movement between the hands. This example shows a ii-V-I progression in C major using these common formulas.

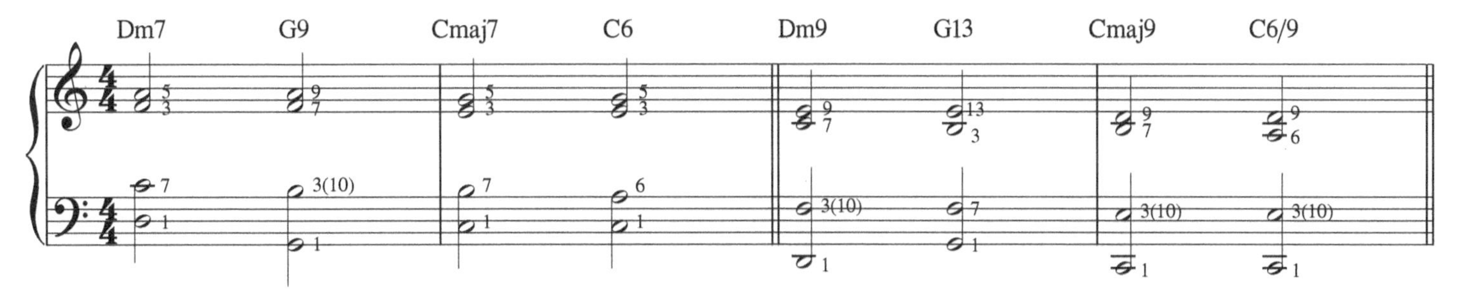

Smooth voice leading also occurs when using left-hand 1-5 voicings with alternating 3-7 and 7-3 right-hand voicings.

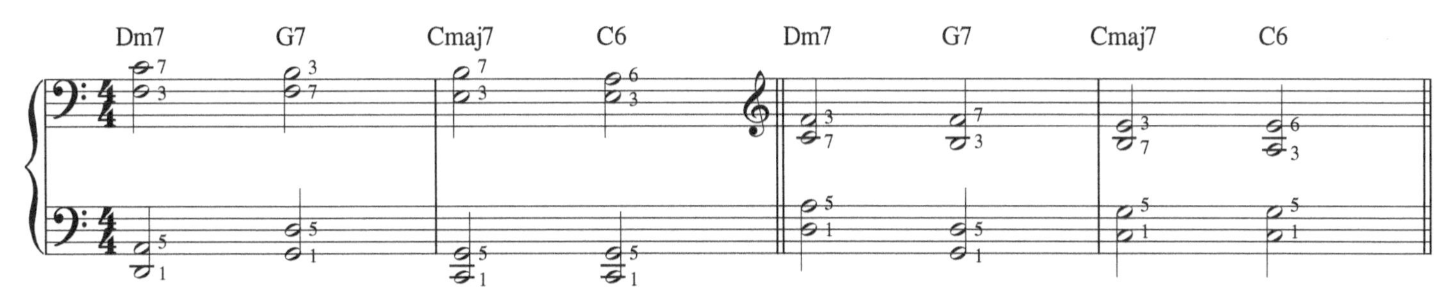

Altered tones are easily adapted to these formulas. This example uses ♭9 and ♭13 for the G7 chords, respectively.

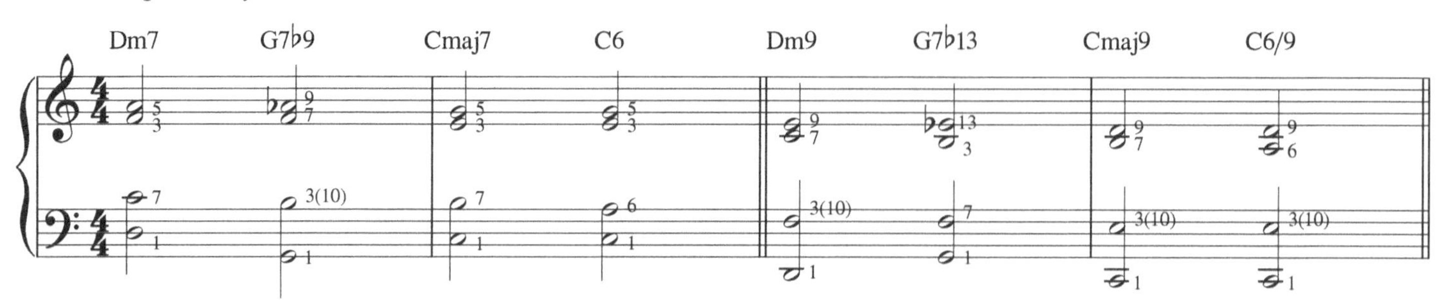

These same formulas can be used in minor keys as well.

Open voicings can be combined in a number of different ways. There are many examples in the chapters that follow. Here are two examples for a ii-V-I progression in F major.

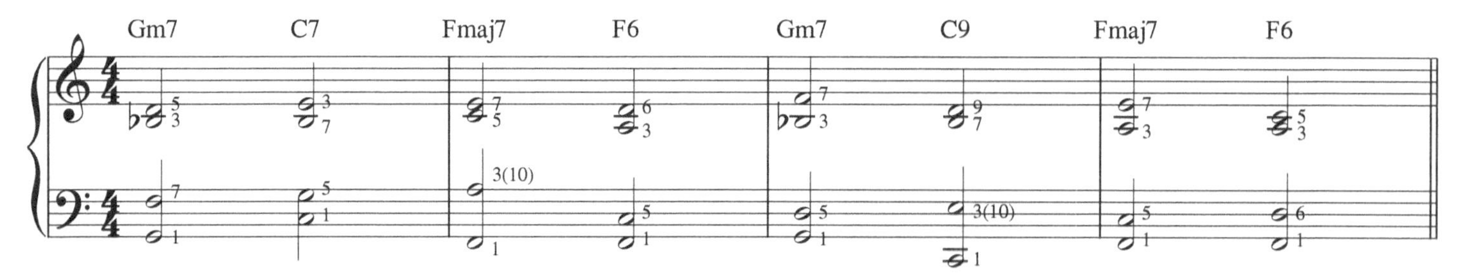

FIVE-NOTE OPEN VOICINGS FOR TWO HANDS

A fifth note can be added to a basic four-note voicing. Some common five-note voicings are given below.

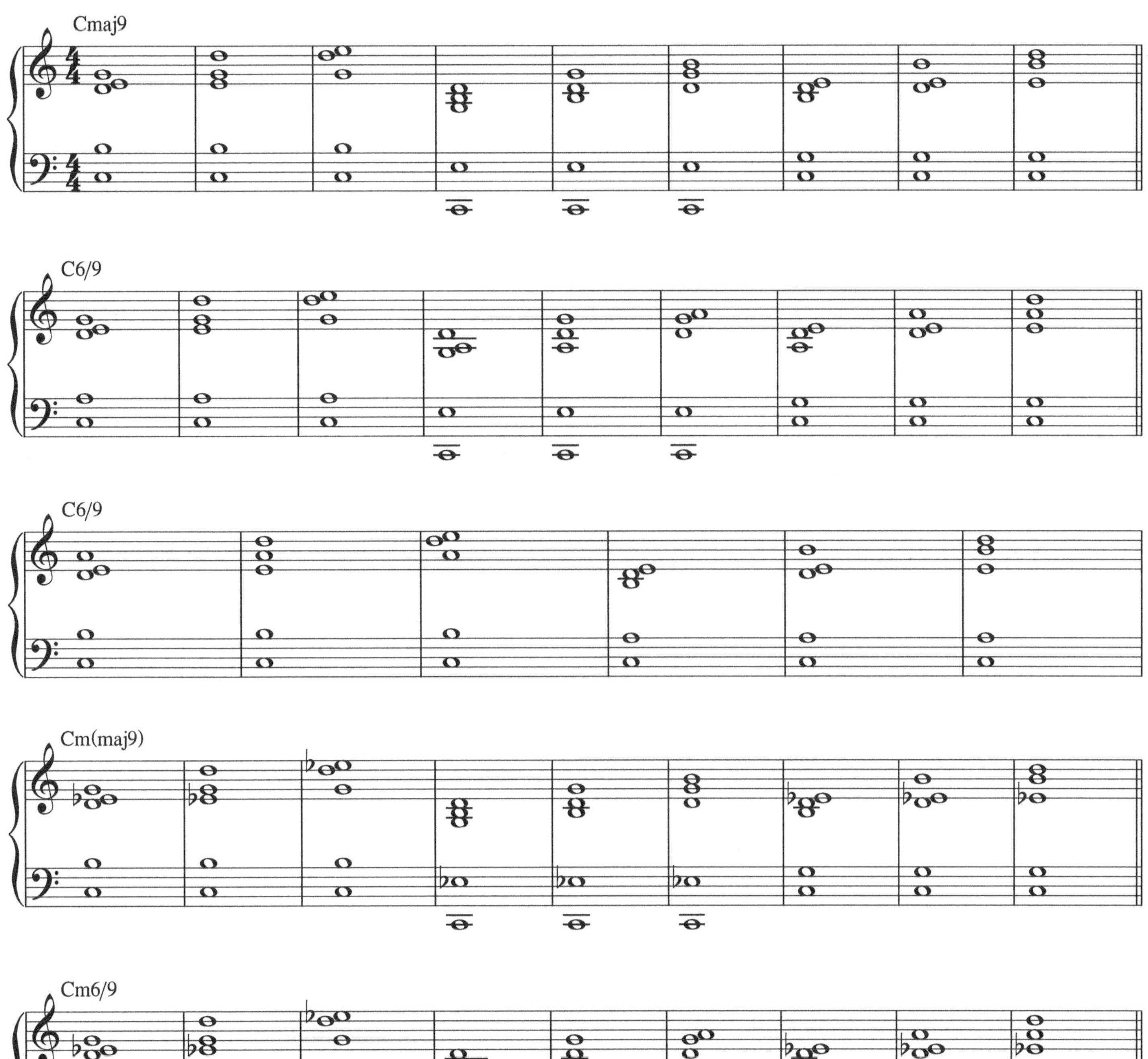

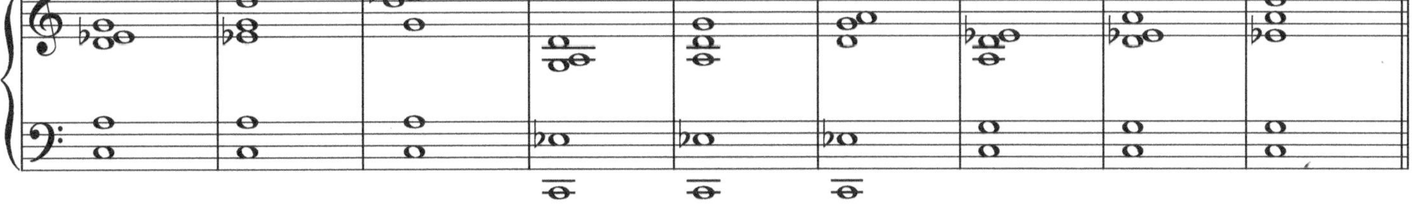

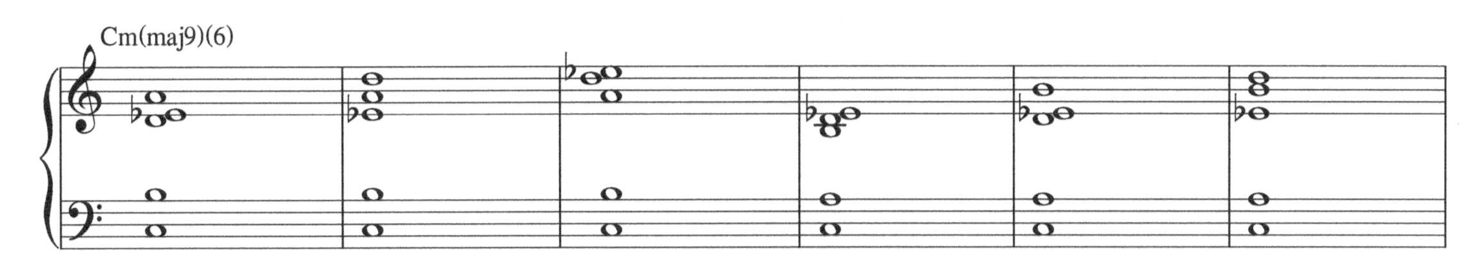

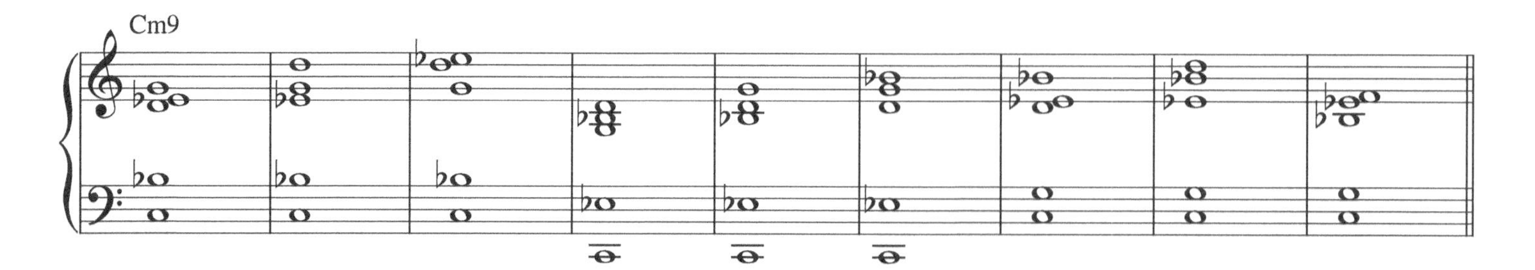
Cm9

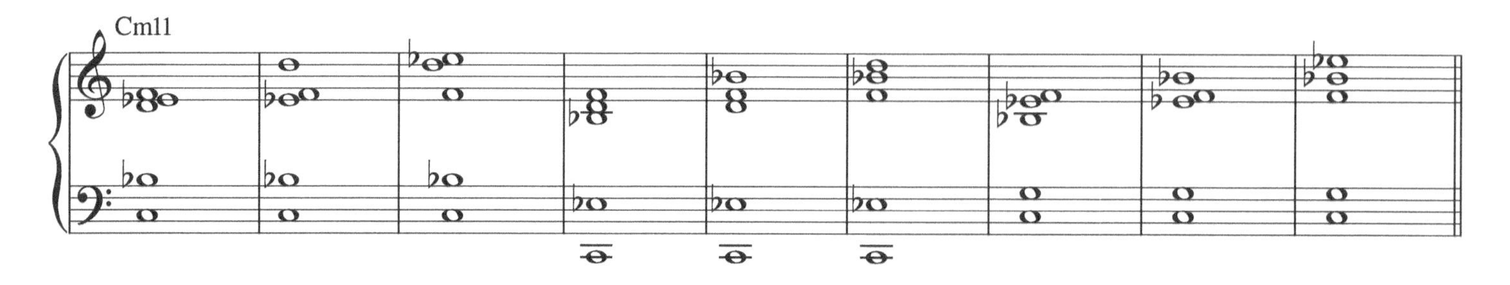
Cm11

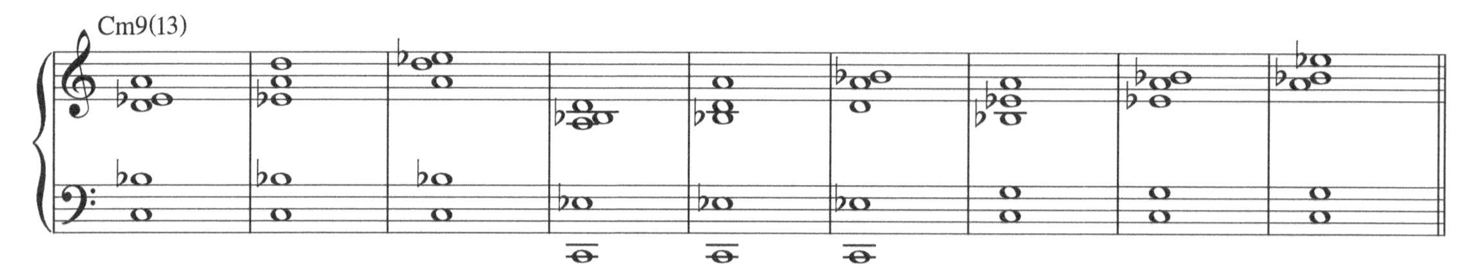
Cm9(13)

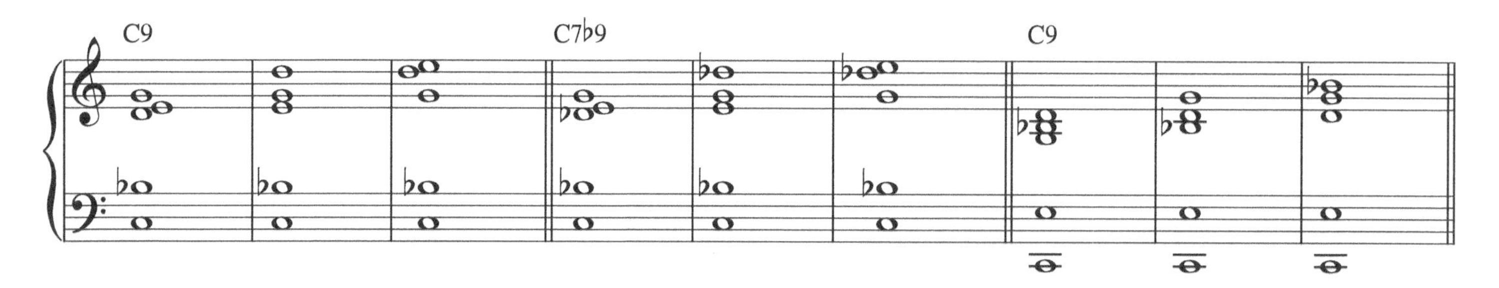
C9
C7♭9
C9

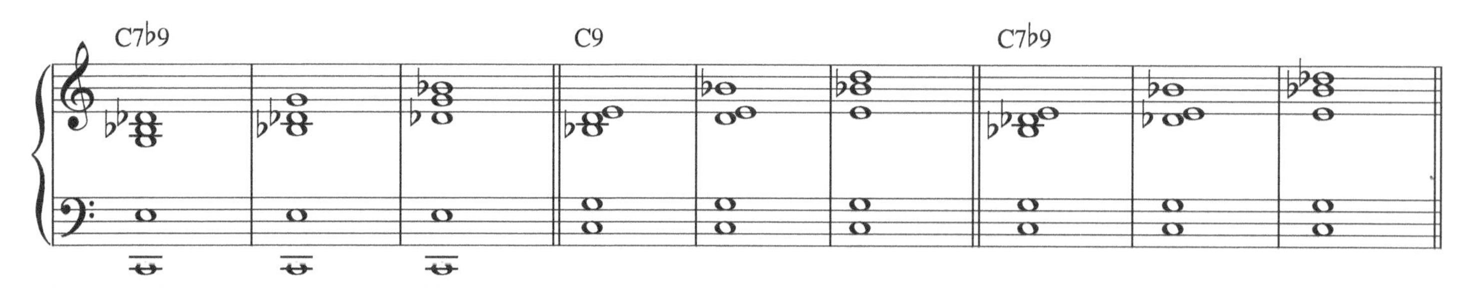
C7♭9
C9
C7♭9

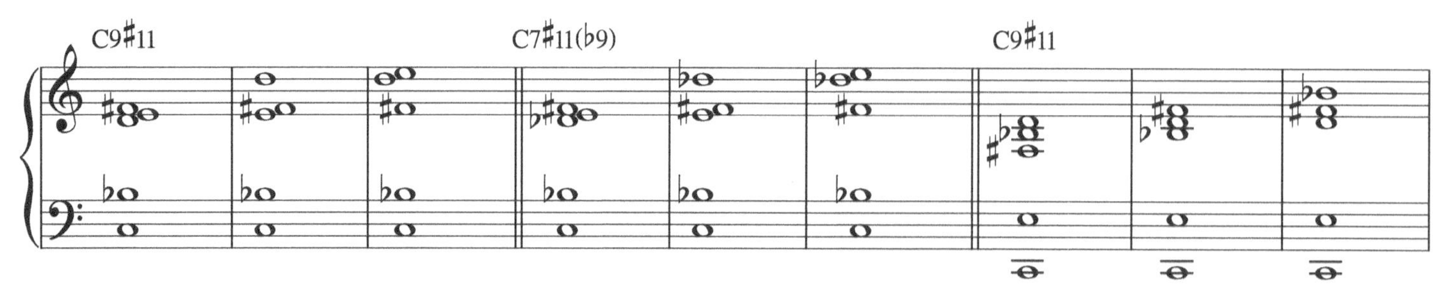
C9♯11
C7♯11(♭9)
C9♯11

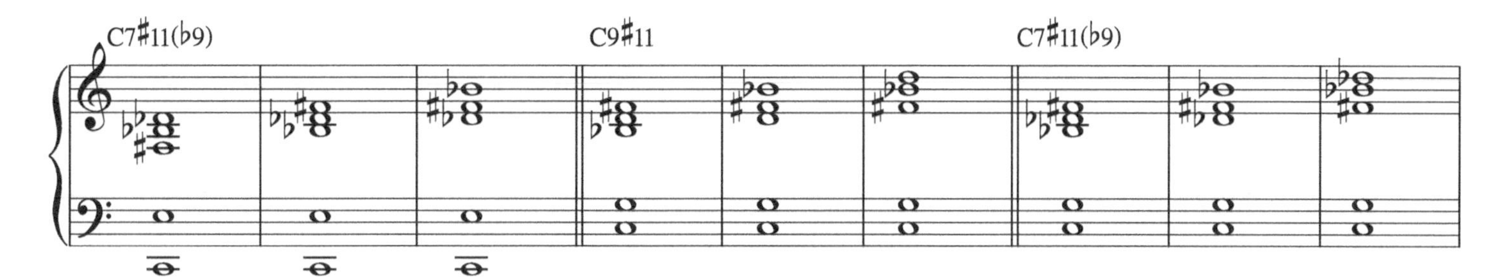
C7♯11(♭9)
C9♯11
C7♯11(♭9)

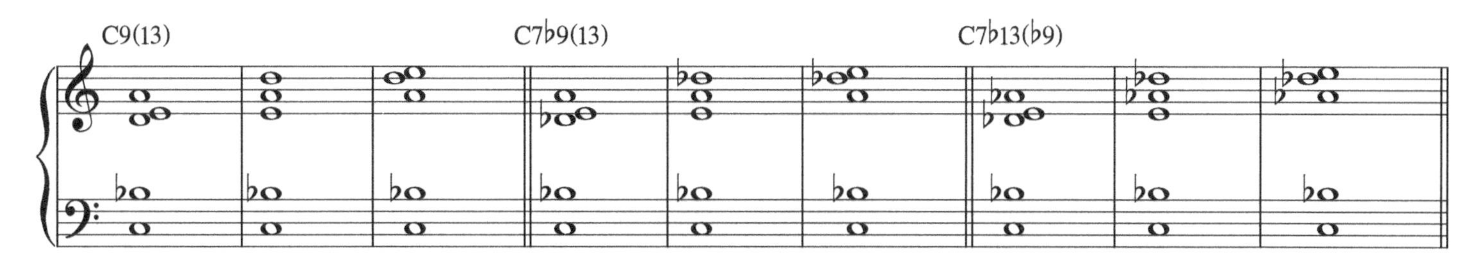
C9(13)
C7♭9(13)
C7♭13(♭9)

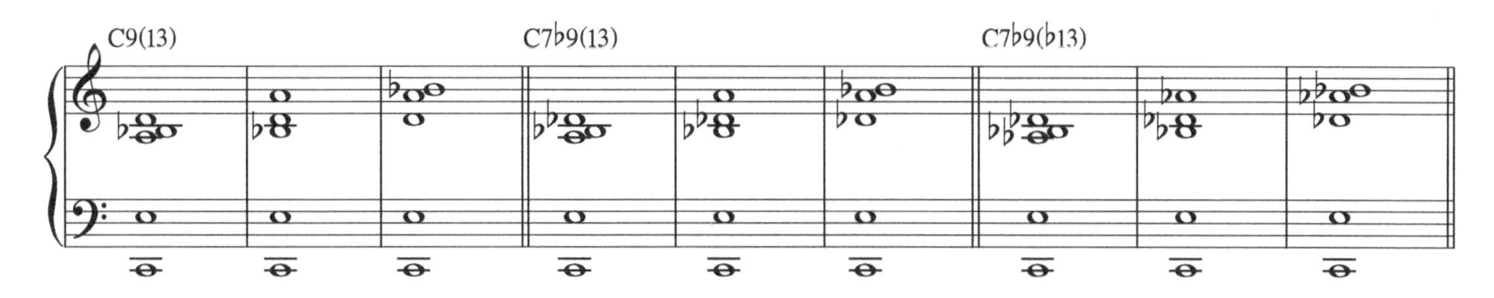
C9(13)
C7♭9(13)
C7♭9(♭13)

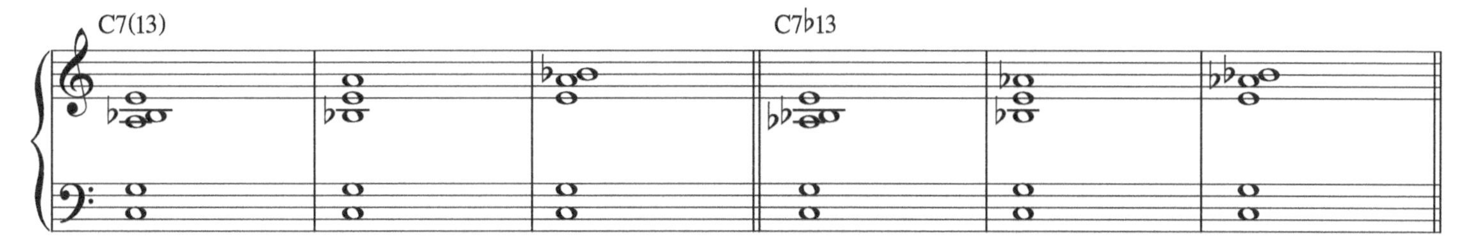
C7(13)
C7♭13

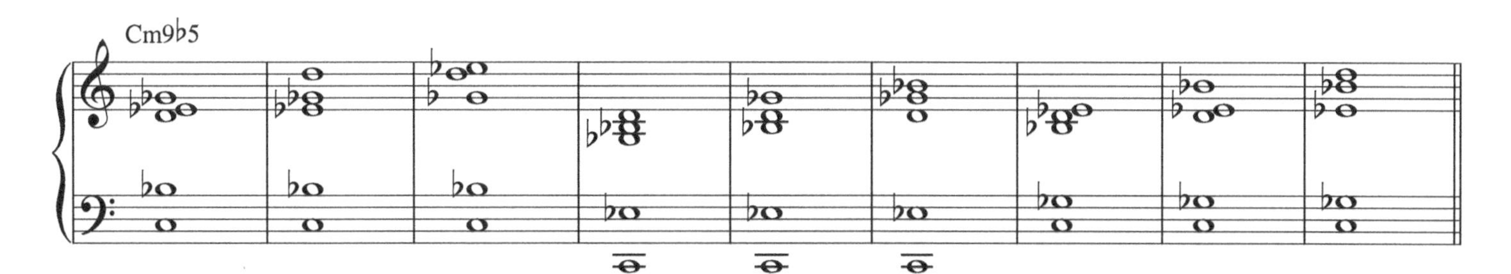
Cm9♭5

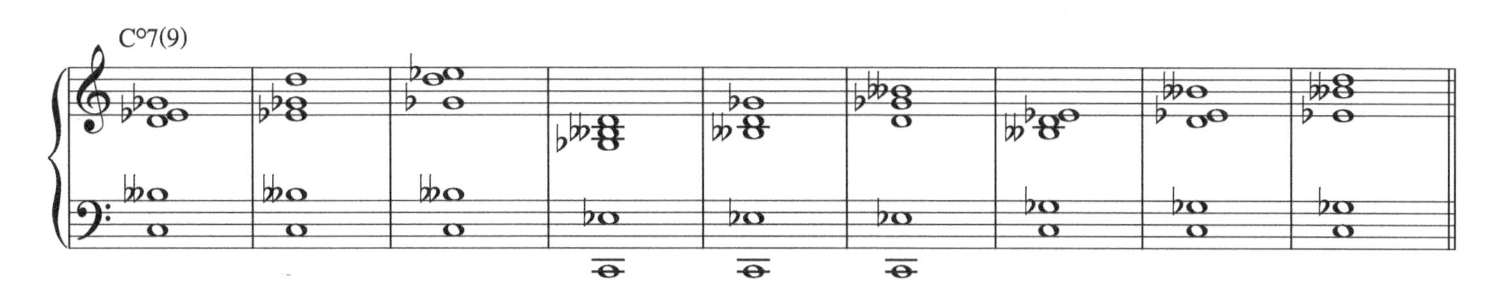
C°7(9)

Five-note voicings can be used for ii-V-I progressions (etc.) by adding the fifth note to the four-note formula voicings. A few examples follow.

As with four-note voicing formulas, altered notes are easily employed with five-note formulas.

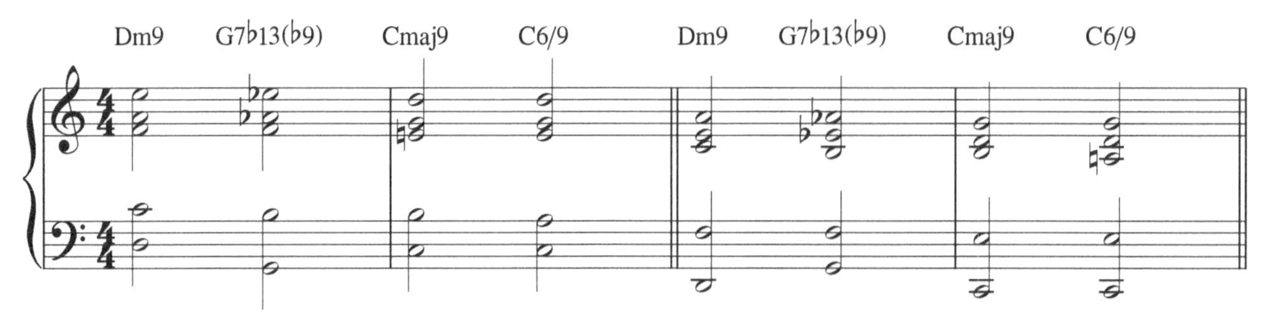

SIX-NOTE OPEN VOICINGS FOR TWO HANDS

There are many possible six-note open voicings. Several examples follow.

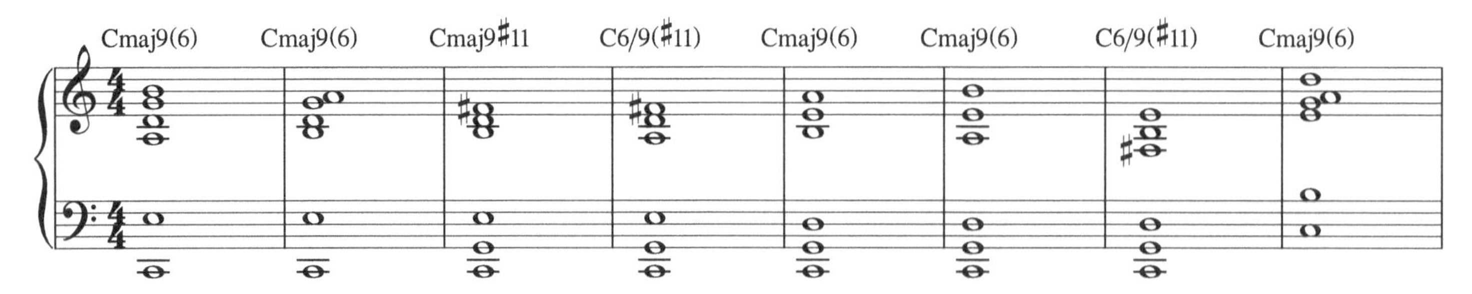

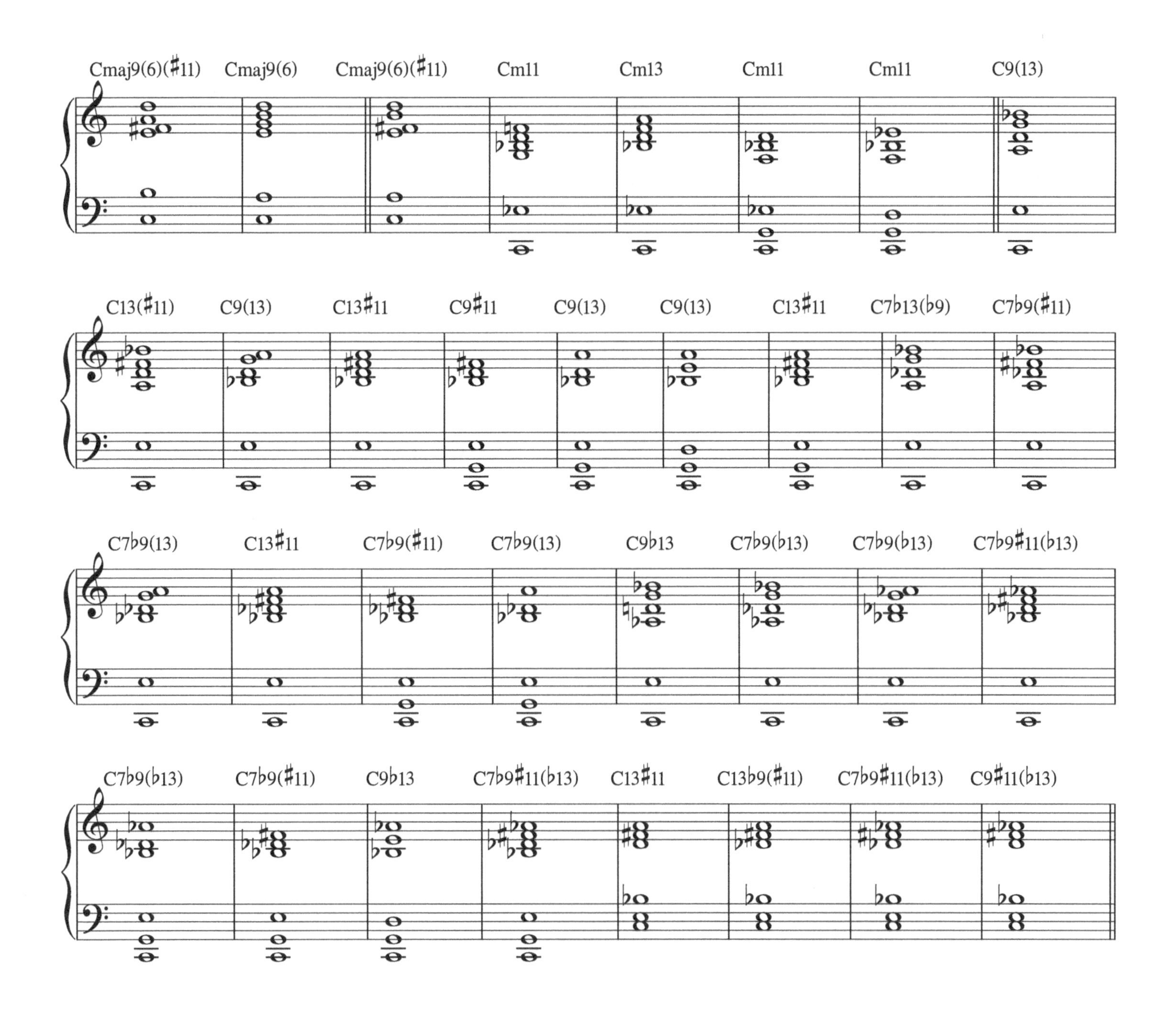

FOUR-NOTE EXTENDED VOICINGS FOR ONE HAND (ROOTLESS VOICINGS)

The following four-note voicings contain no roots, for the most part, and are typically played in the left hand when performing with a bass player. By letting go of the root, the pianist can easily play extended chord tones in its place. Although solo pianists usually play the roots of chords in a bassist's absence, these mostly rootless voicings are usefully played in the left hand before or after the root, and in the right hand while filling the harmony – along with the melody on top of a left-hand bass part.

Below are some commonly used four-note voicings with the root C. Even though they are written in the right-hand staff above the root, they should be learned in both hands. The first group lists voicings that have the third of the chord as the lowest note – except one voicing for a Cm7♭5 chord that begins on the root. The chord tones used for each chord quality are as follows.

Major 7th: 3-5-7-9
Major 6th: 3-5-6-9
Minor (major7): 3-5-7-9
Minor 6th: 3-5-6-9

Minor 7th: 3-5-7-9
Minor 7th♭5: 3-5-7-9, 3-5-7-♭9, 3-5-7-8, 1-4-5-7
Dominant 7th: 3-13-7-9, altered notes are similar
Diminished 7th: 3-5-7-9

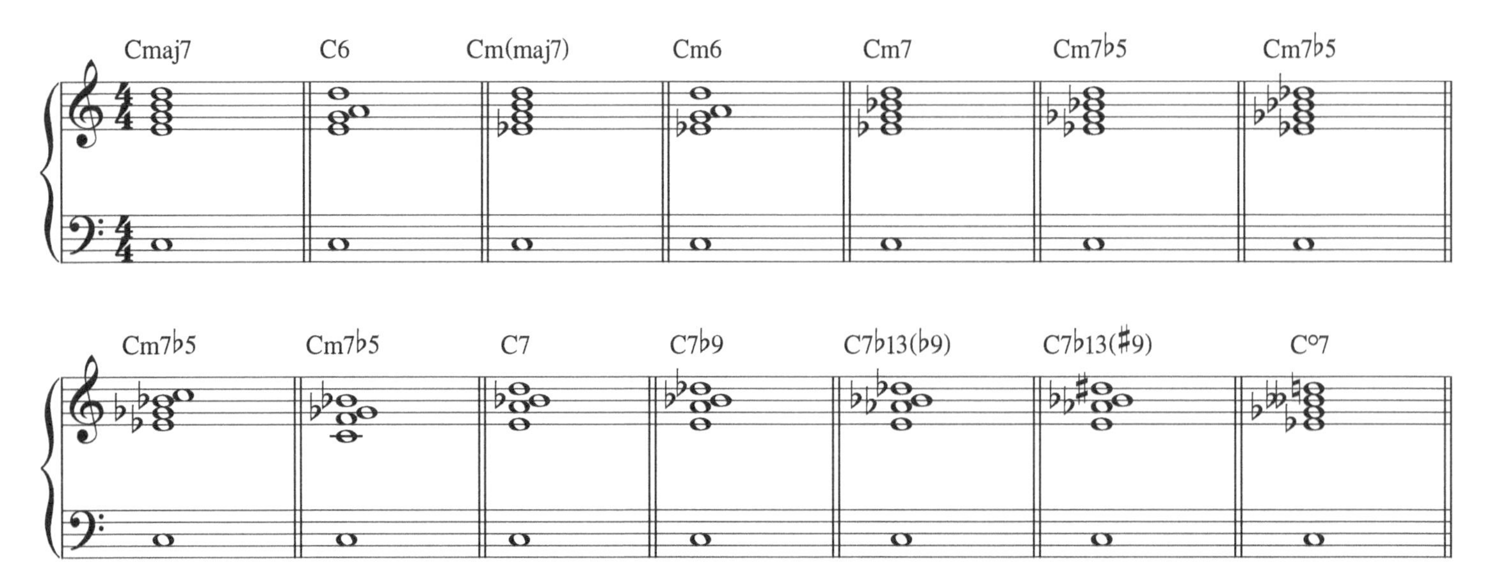

The voicings in this next group begin with the seventh or sixth as the lowest note. The chord tones used for each chord quality are as follows.

Major 7th: 7-9-3-5, 7-8-3-5
Major 6th: 6-9-3-5
Minor (major7): 7-9-3-5
Minor 6th: 6-9-3-5
Minor 7th: 7-9-3-5,
Minor 7♭5: 7-9-3-5, 7-♭9-3-5
Dominant 7th: 7-9-3-5, altered notes are similar
Diminished 7th: 7-9-3-5

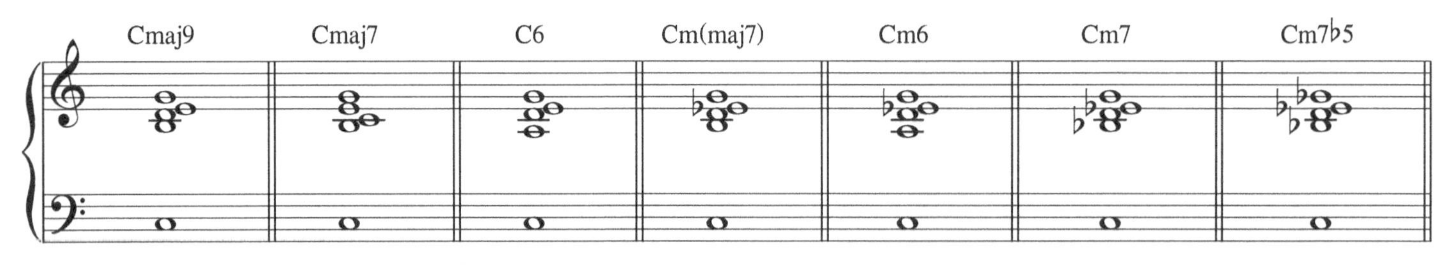

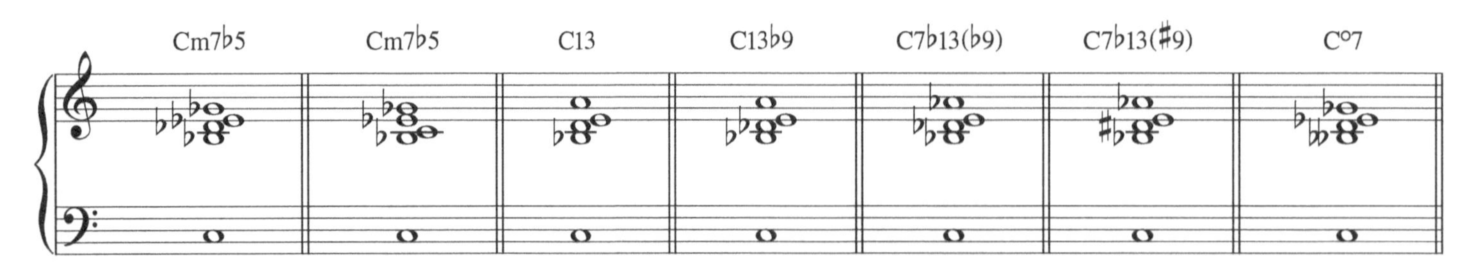

The four-note voicings are used time and again in sequences that alternate voicings from each of the groups above. This follows the guide-tone principle used in voicing formulas we saw earlier. Notice the third of one chord leading to the seventh of the succeeding chord. Two examples for a ii-V-I progression in C major are shown below. Some theorists refer to these formulas and the voicings within each as the A and B forms, respectively.

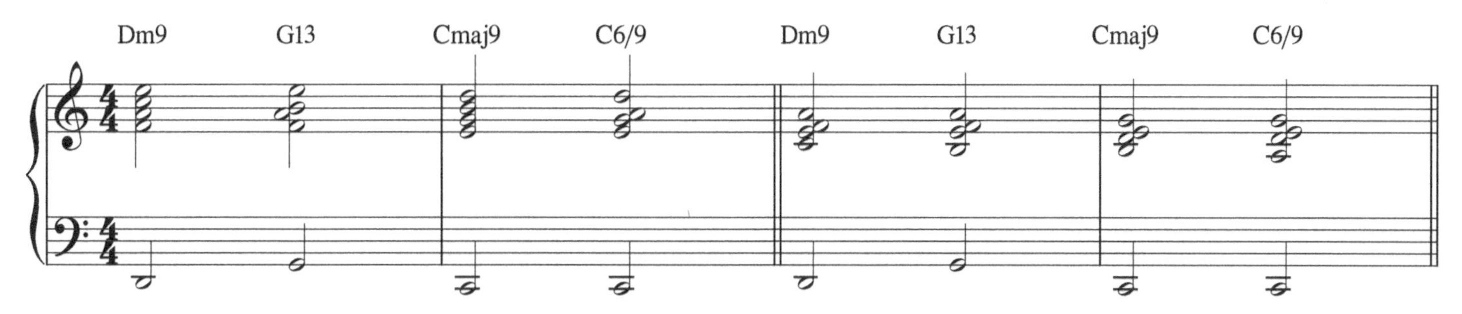

THREE-NOTE EXTENDED VOICINGS FOR ONE HAND

Three-note versions of the four-note voicings shown above are constructed by leaving out a note. They have an open sound and are useful when such a sonority is desired. Ideally, the pianist should vary sounds and textures by using both open- and close-position voicings.

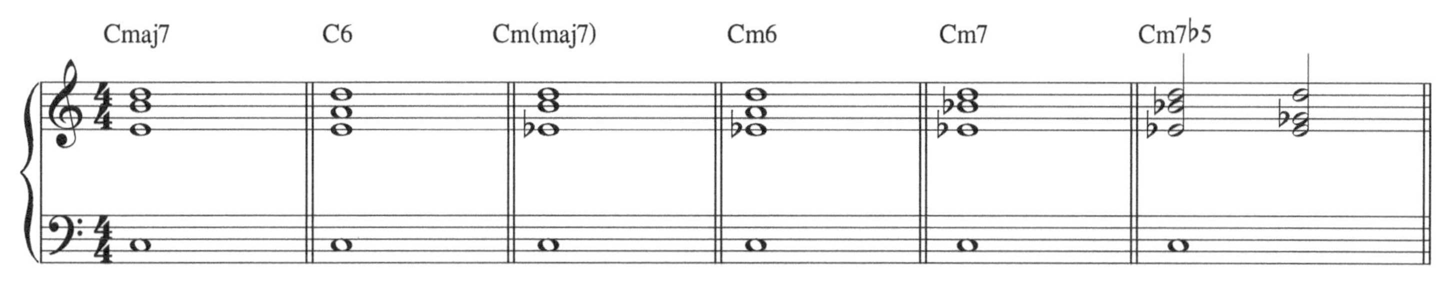

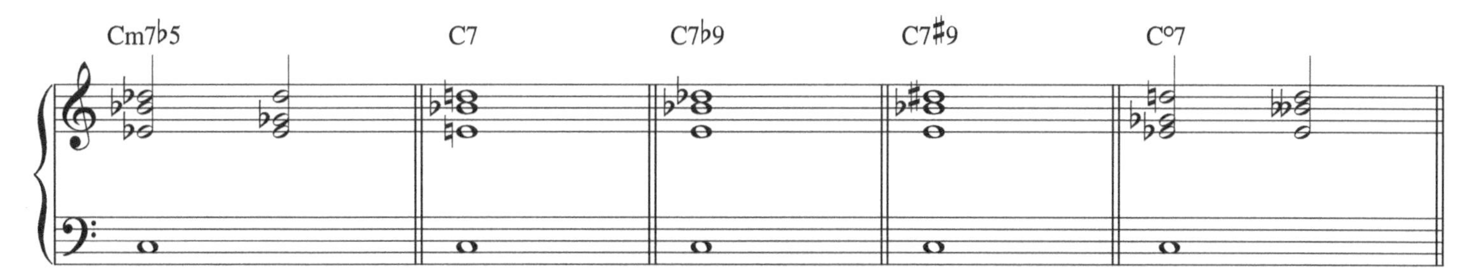

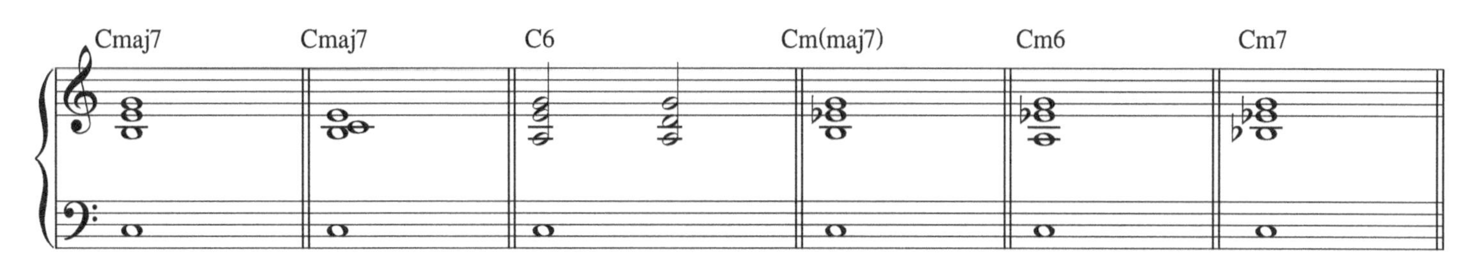

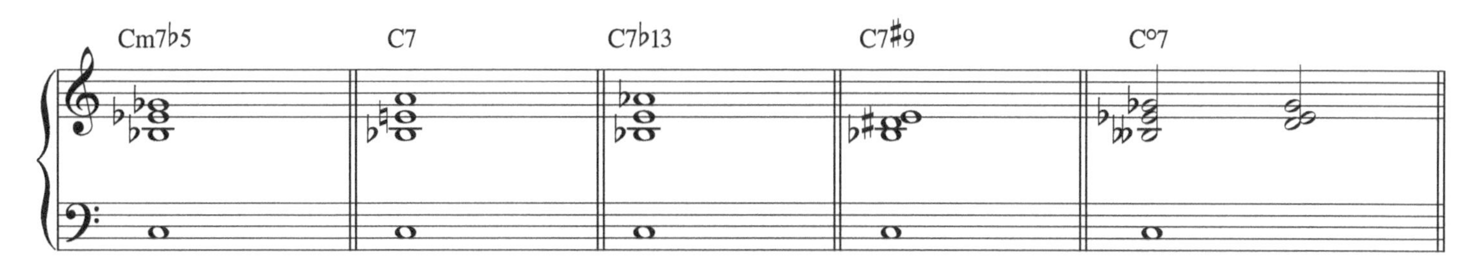

These three-note voicings are generally coupled according to guide tones, as are the four-note versions. Examples for a ii-V-I progression in C major are shown below.

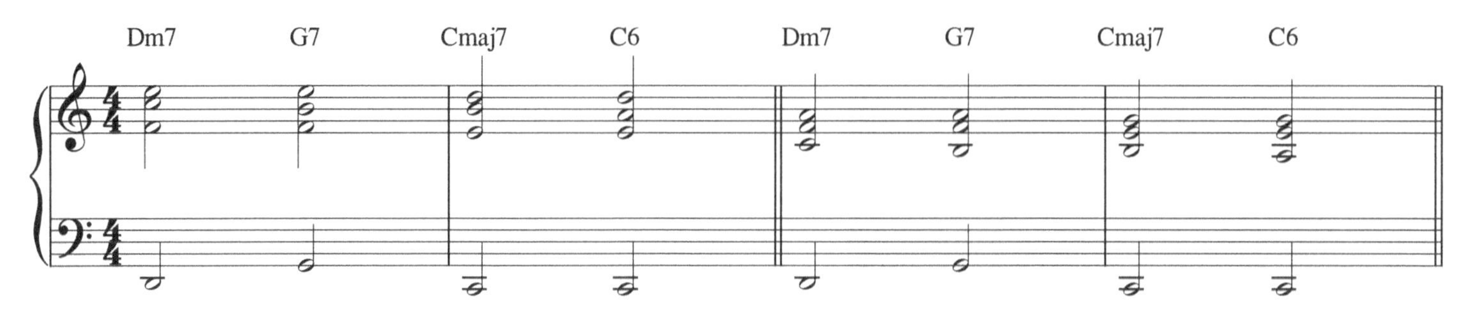

The next and succeeding chapters will offer numerous examples of putting all the above voicings into practical use.

CHAPTER 2
VOICING TUNES

VOICING WITH TWO HANDS

We pianists can best get inside a tune by isolating the harmony, bass, and melody from each other. Harmonically, we should practice a tune by voicing the chords alone in several ways by using different voicings and voicing systems or formulas before applying them to the melody itself. Ideally, we should have as many options as possible literally on the tips of our fingers. The following examples are for the first eight measures of "Winter Comes."

Close-Position Seventh Chords in Right Hand with Roots in the Left Hand

The following excerpts employ close-position seventh chords with smooth voice leading.

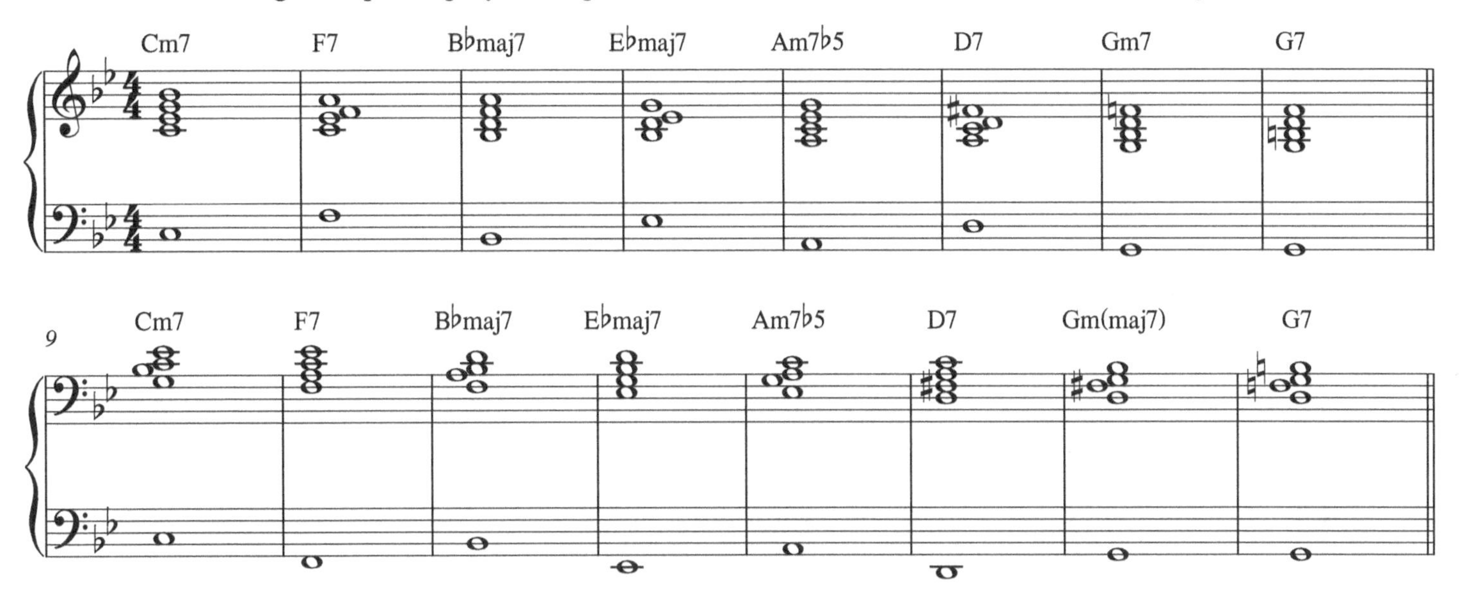

Close-Position Seventh Chords in Left Hand with Right-Hand Melody

Track 1

Rootless Right-Hand Voicings with Left-Hand Roots

The following examples make use of rootless voicing formulas.

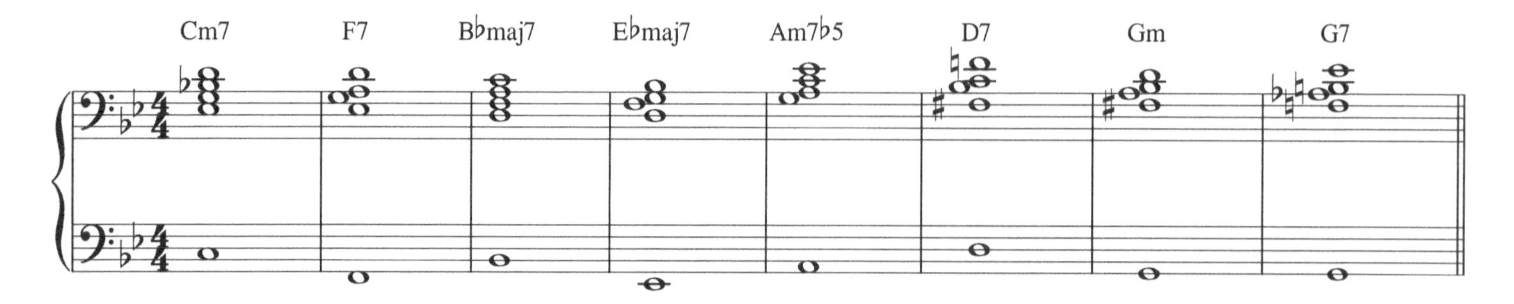

Rootless Left-Hand Voicings with Right-Hand Melody

Track 2

Cm7 F7 B♭maj7 E♭maj7 Am7♭5 D7 Gm G7

You can also sound the roots of the left-hand voicings playing before the voicings themselves.

Right-Hand Melody and Chords with Left-Hand Roots

Voice chord tones below the melody note at each new chord change. Rootless voicings add color to the harmony; roots are unnecessary in the right hand since the left hand is playing them.

Track 4

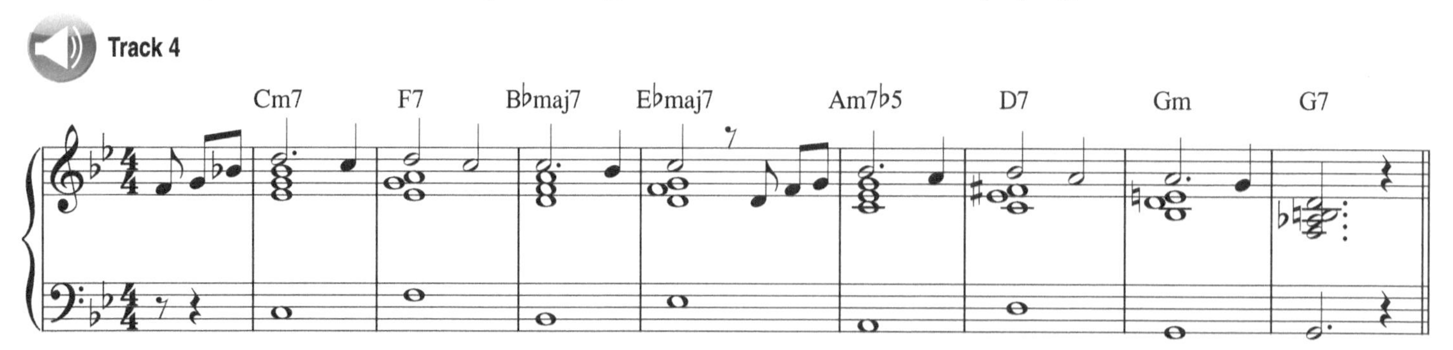

Right-Hand Melody with Left-Hand Three-Note Voicings

Play the melody with three-note root-position chords in the left hand. These voicings can be 1-3-7 or 1-7-10. The 1-7-10 voicing is not always practical because of the large stretch involved in reaching some of the tenths. If you have difficulty with any tenth intervals, simply play 1-3-7.

Swing Feel with Three-Note Voicings

Try a swing version of "Winter Comes" by changing the melodic rhythm while comping three-note chords in the left hand.

Left-Hand Guide Tones

Guide tones are simple yet effective voicing formulas that give just enough harmonic information without cluttering up the texture. They contain only the third and seventh (or sixth) of each chord and move smoothly, alternating 3-7 and 7-3 of each chord when the root movement in down a fifth. They are especially useful during up-tempo improvisations. Practice these by themselves and then with roots either before or after them.

Open Voicings with Both Hands

Practice the chords of a tune using open voicings and open-voicing formulas. Three examples for the first eight measures of "Winter Comes" follow.

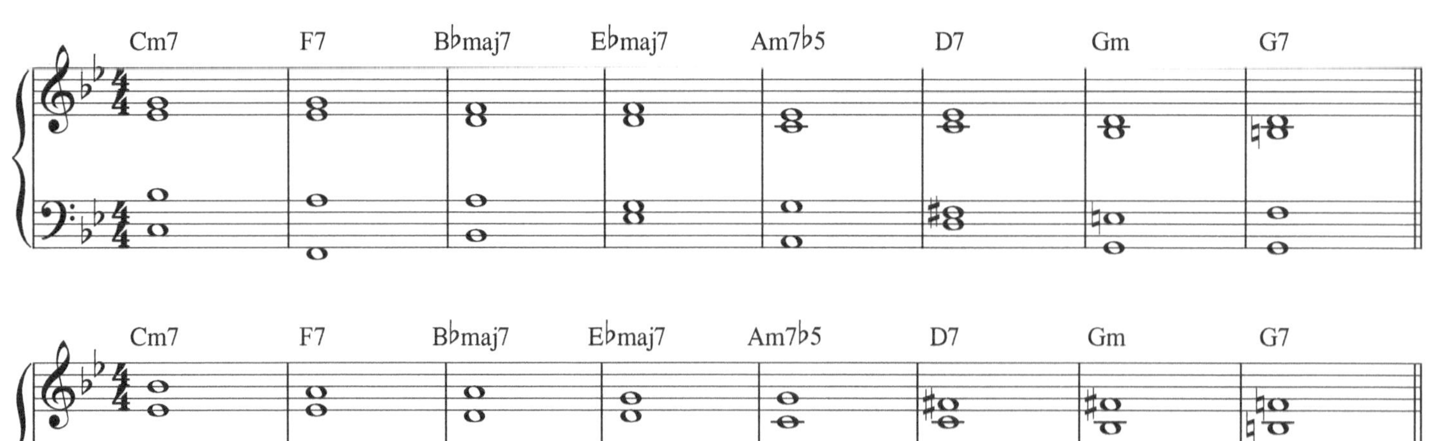

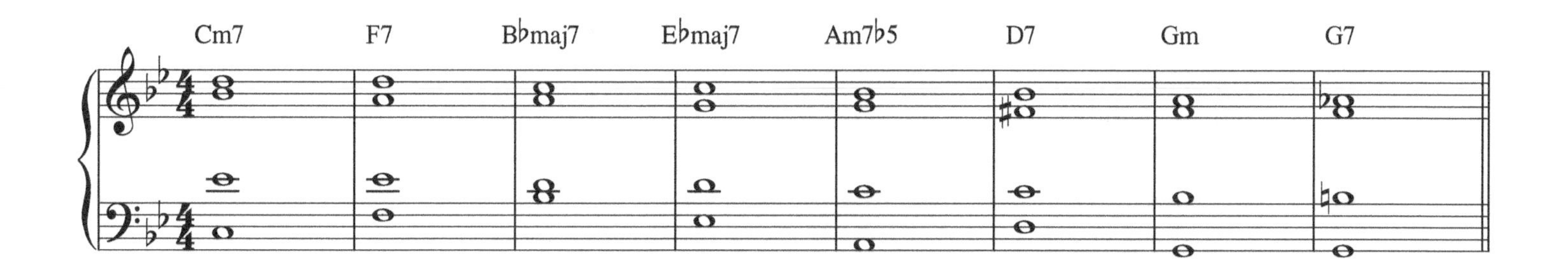

Melody with Open Voicings

Now play the melody using each voicing formula.

Track 8

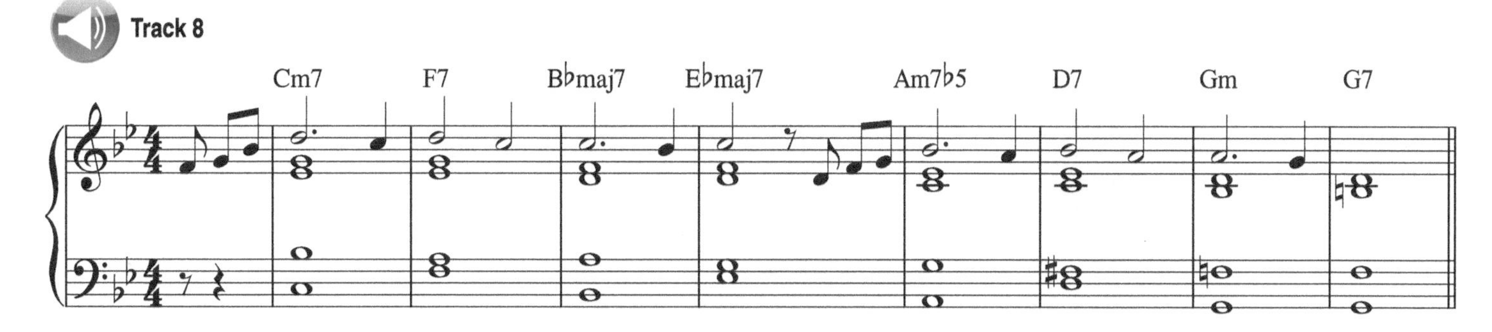

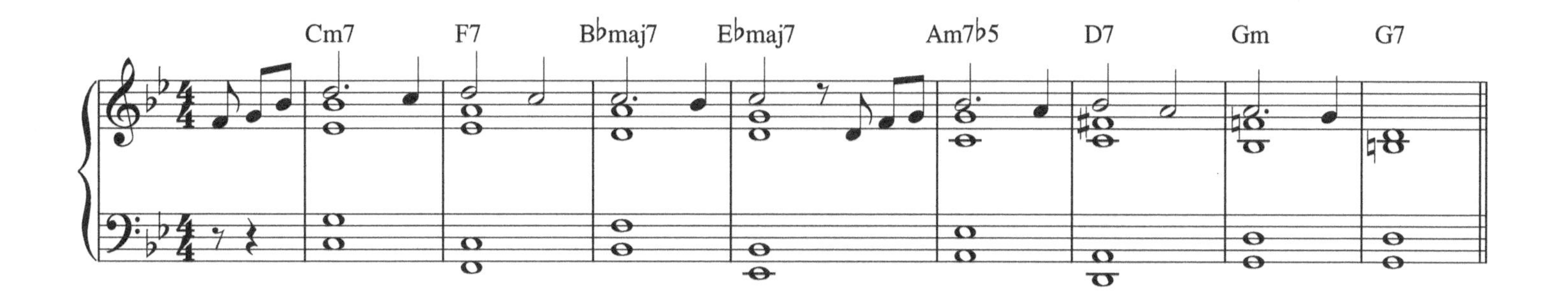

"Winter Comes" with Mixed Open Voicings

Next, play melody and chords using various open voicings and open-voicing formulas. You will find certain voicings work better than others depending on where the melody lies and the register of the chords. There is no single way to do this; try many alternatives. A complete version of "Winter Comes" follows.

Displaced Bass with Open Voicings

Sometimes the root of the chord is separated from the rest of the voicing. This process can add extra rhythmic impetus to the music. The displaced voicing can be set anywhere within the harmonic frame. The tune's melody and style are the best indicators of where the displacement should occur. The following example uses a simple half-note rhythm.

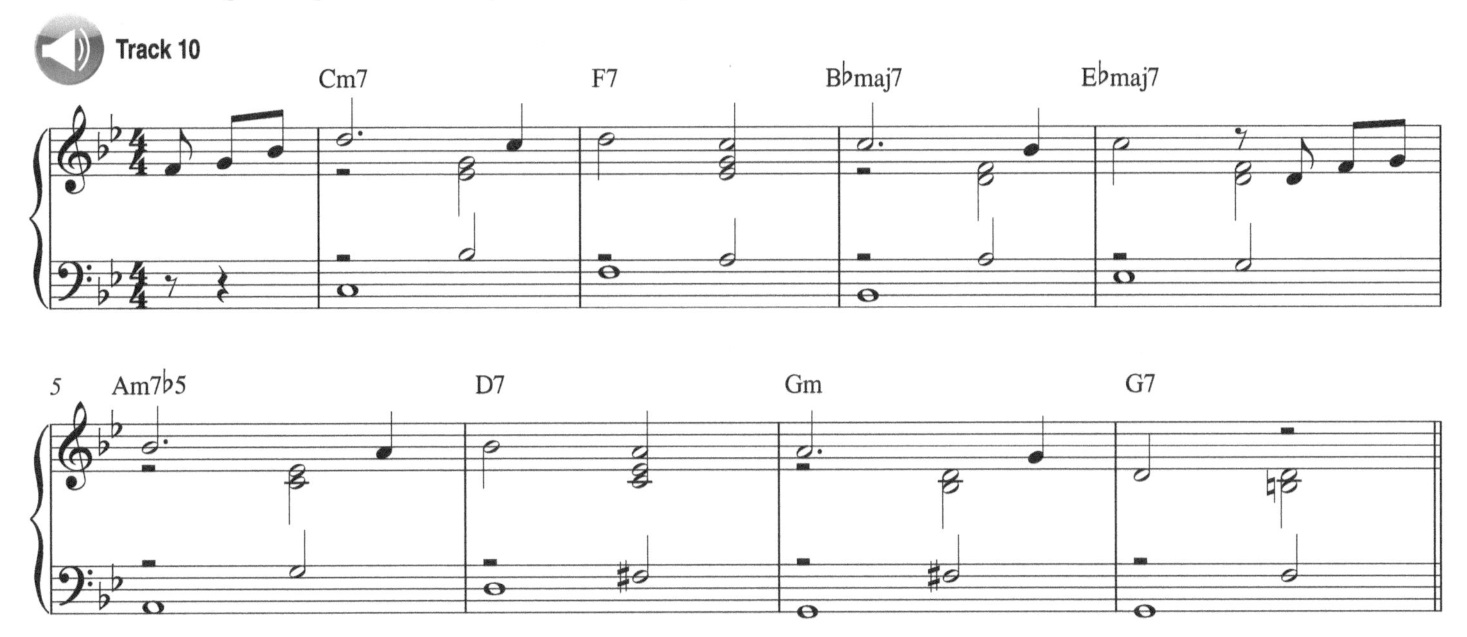

MIXING VOICINGS AND RHYTHMIC PLACEMENT

Ideally, the solo pianist should play with a variety of voicings while rhythmically activating the melody and chords. As stated above, the rhythmic placement of chords depends on the style or feel of the music. Be aware of the composite rhythm among the parts and avoid unnecessary rhythmic redundancies. The following example is a swing version of the first half of "Winter Comes." The chords are comped in between melody notes as often as the music allows.

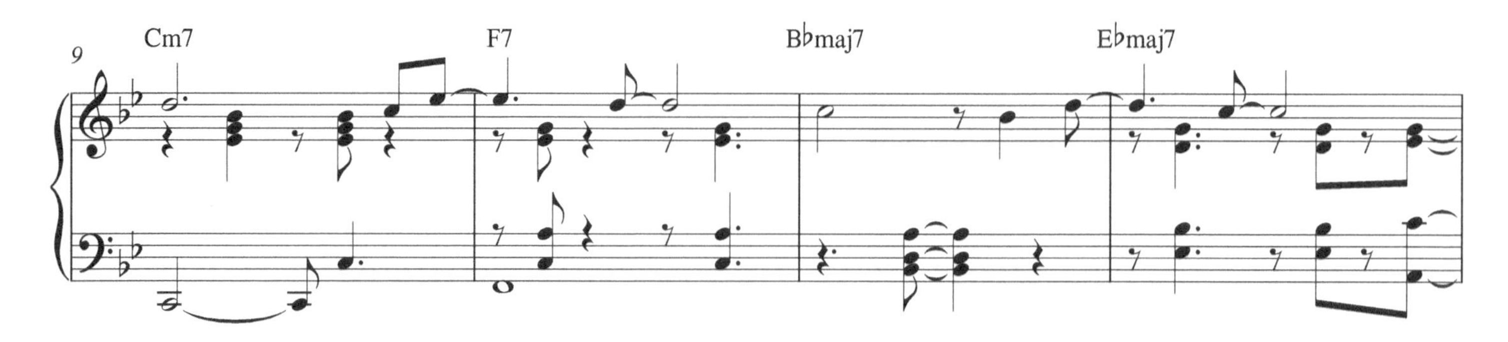
9
Cm7
F7
B♭maj7
E♭maj7

13
Am7♭5
D7
Gm

CHAPTER 3
BASS LINES

Tunes, for the most part, function on three different layers simultaneously: melody, harmony, and bass. The trick to solo piano playing is to make all three layers audible; the difficulty lies in presenting the three layers with only two hands. All three layers, however, can be implied throughout a performance and the skilled pianist can give the illusion that all are being heard. We can play a bass line at the expense of the chord changes or the chords in lieu of the bass line, but we can also refer to each layer enough that the listener misses neither. Whether or not we choose to play bass lines during a performance, we should be aware of potential bass lines, because root and bass motion are inherent in the tune and offer avenues for harmonic and melodic exploration.

HALF-NOTE BASS LINES

The simplest way to play a bass part is to sound the root of each chord – or occasionally another chord tone, when an inversion is structurally important. Play a bass note for each new chord; that's the first step to abstracting the bass from a tune. Below are the first eight measures of "Winter Comes." Play all of "Winter Comes" in a similar manner (page 32).

When chords last for four or more beats, a bass line consisting of half notes can be constructed by playing the fifth of each chord after the root.

The third of each chord can follow the root as well as the fifth. The bass line below uses thirds and fifths for measures 9-16 of "Autumn Comes."

It is helpful to think of **target notes** as goals within bass lines. Although roots of chords are most often used as target notes, other chord tones can be enlisted as well. Approaching a chord root (or any target note) by half step above or below is a standard technique in playing bass lines. These notes are called **leading tones** and generally work even when they are not part of the prevailing chord. It gives the impression of leaning into the next note and adds a sense of forward motion to the bass line. Notice this effect on the beginning of "Winter Comes."

Track 15

Mixing chord tones with leading tones adds variety and non-predictability to a bass line. The second half of "Winter Comes" combines these elements.

Track 16

Experiment with different half-note bass lines on "Winter Comes" and on some standard tunes such as "Autumn Leaves," "All the Things You Are," "Fly Me to the Moon," et al.

WALKING BASS

Walking bass usually refers to a bass line comprised mostly of quarter notes. There is a variety of ways to construct these. Play roots and fifths; that's one simple way. The following example uses a ii-V-I progression in C major.

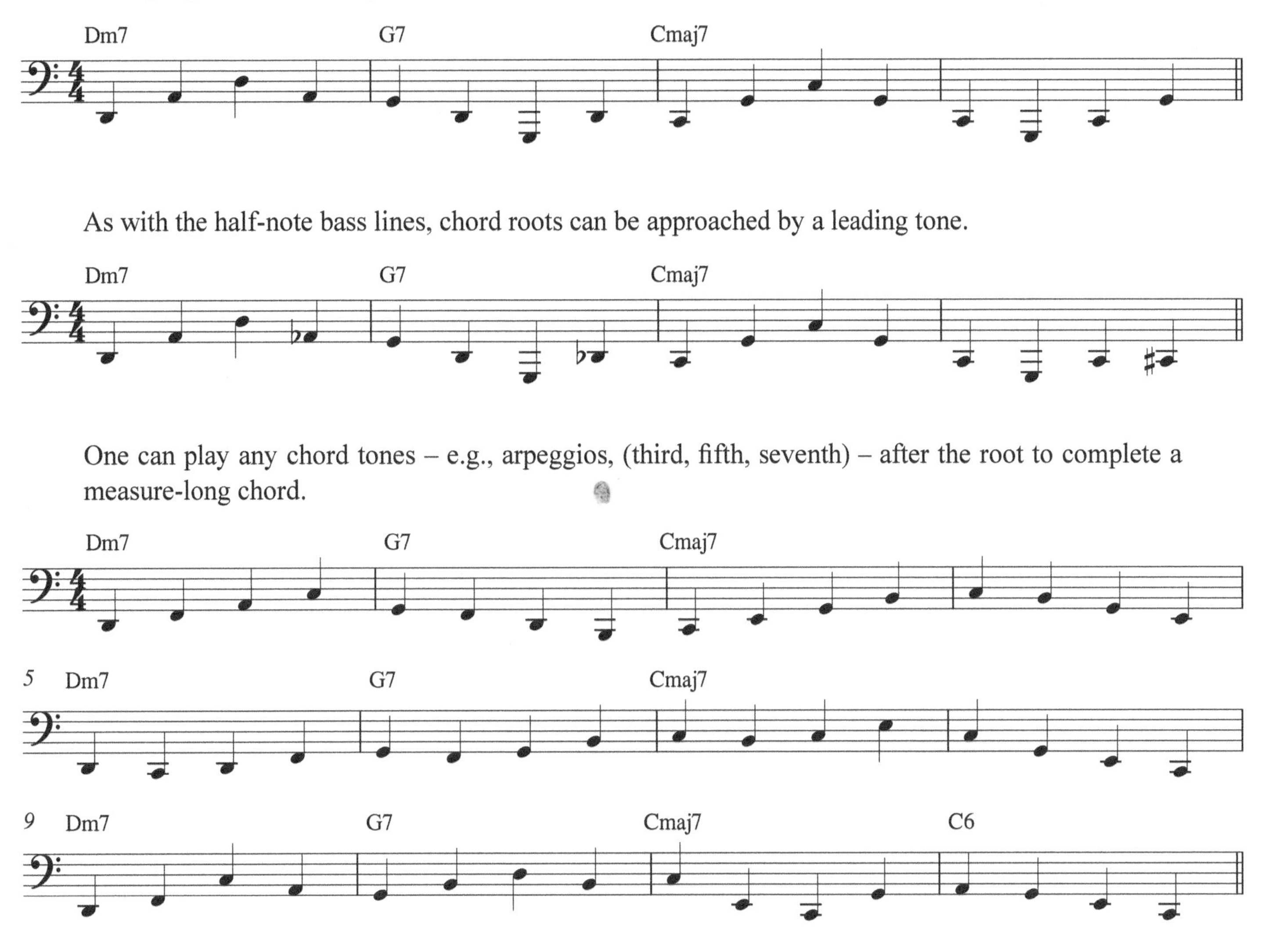

As with the half-note bass lines, chord roots can be approached by a leading tone.

One can play any chord tones – e.g., arpeggios, (third, fifth, seventh) – after the root to complete a measure-long chord.

Here is an arpeggiated walking bass line for the beginning of "Winter Comes."

Leading tones are often combined with arpeggiated lines to give the bass line more forward motion. Here are some examples for a ii-V-I progression in C major.

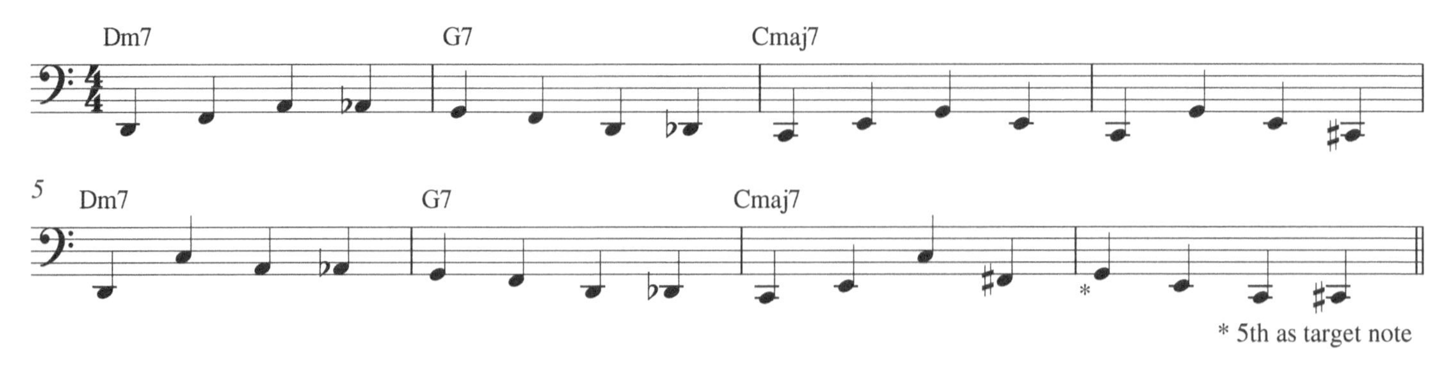

Here is a similar process for the beginning of "Winter Comes."

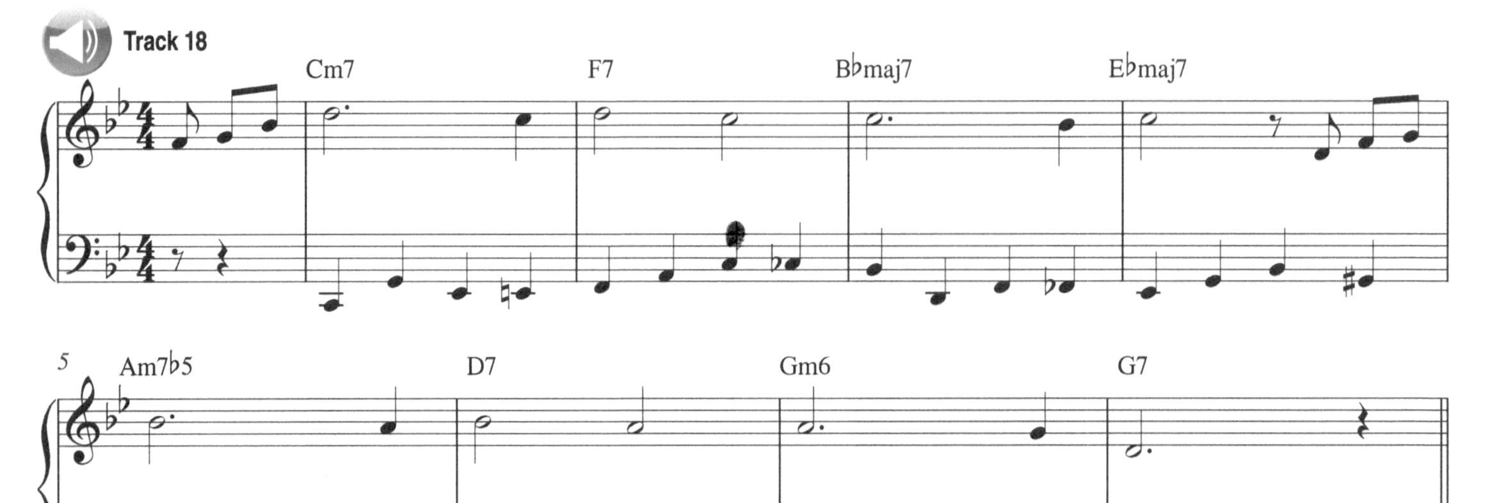

Walking Bass with Stepwise Lines

Stepwise bass lines are constructed by using diatonic and chromatic passing tones and neighbor notes. As long as the target notes are clear for each new chord, we can choose to get to them in various ways through step-wise motion.

Diatonic scale notes can connect target notes that are fifth apart. The following example is a ii-V-I progression in C major; notes of the C major scale are used to create a stepwise bass line. Notes that are not part of the chords are passing tones (PT).

Chromatic passing tones (CPT) can be combined with diatonic passing tones and leading tones (LT) to create goal-directed bass lines. Leading tones and chromatic passing tones often perform the same function. The ii-V-I progression below reverses the direction of the bass line above; chromatic passing tones must be used to preserve the stepwise motion since the target notes are now only a fourth apart.

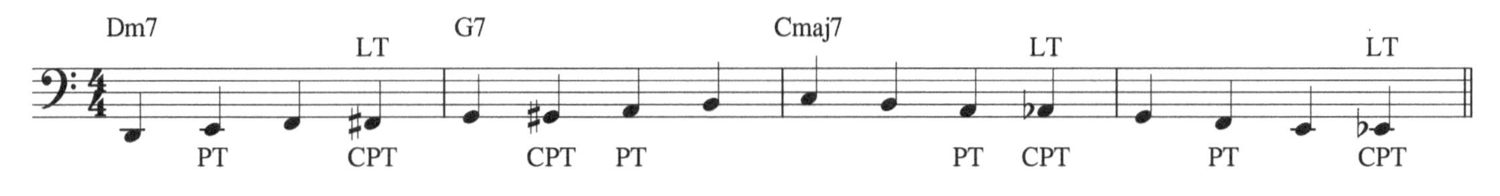

The following ii-V-I progression uses some skips along with passing tones.

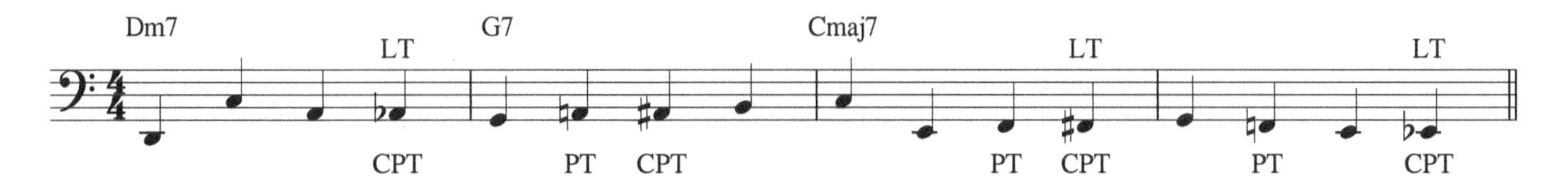

Upper or lower neighbor notes (NN) create motion while focusing on certain notes by moving a step away then back to the original note. This example incorporates a few neighbor notes within the bass line.

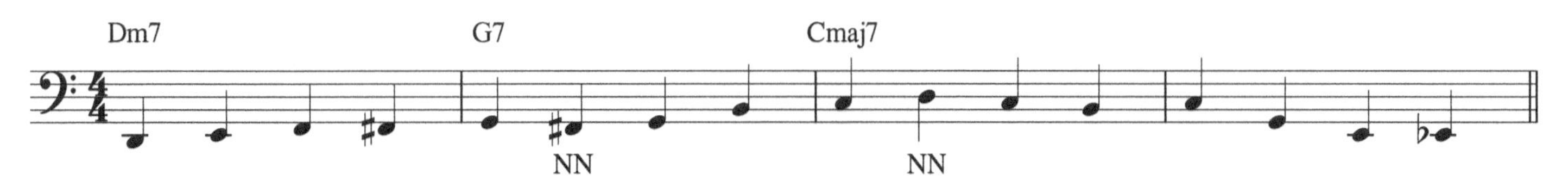

When a chord's duration is that of a half note, apply the same principles used for half-note bass lines shown above. The following example is based on a variation of a blues progression.

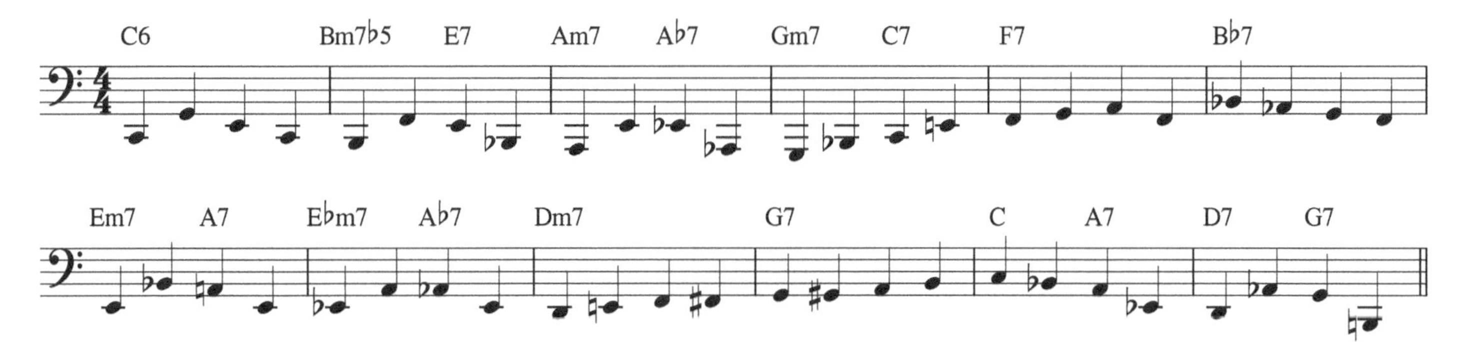

"Winter Comes" with Walking Bass

This walking bass line for "Winter Comes" uses all the techniques described above. The right hand plays the melody.

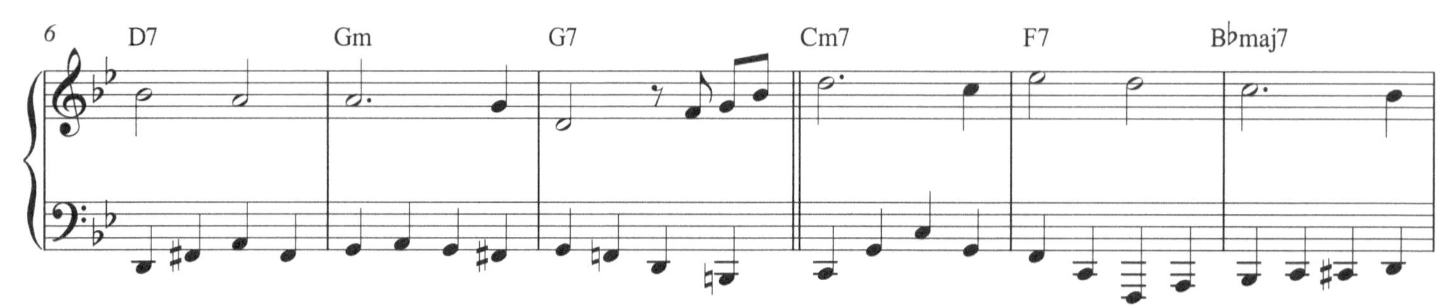

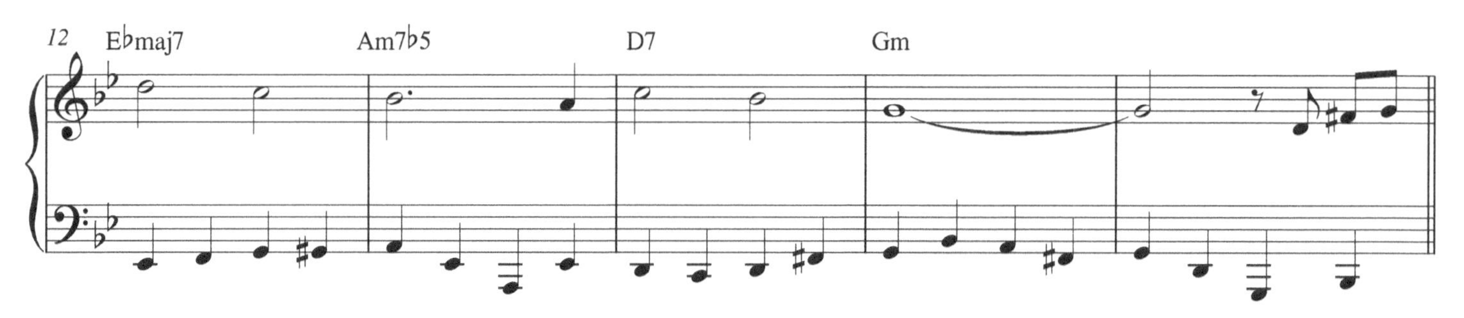

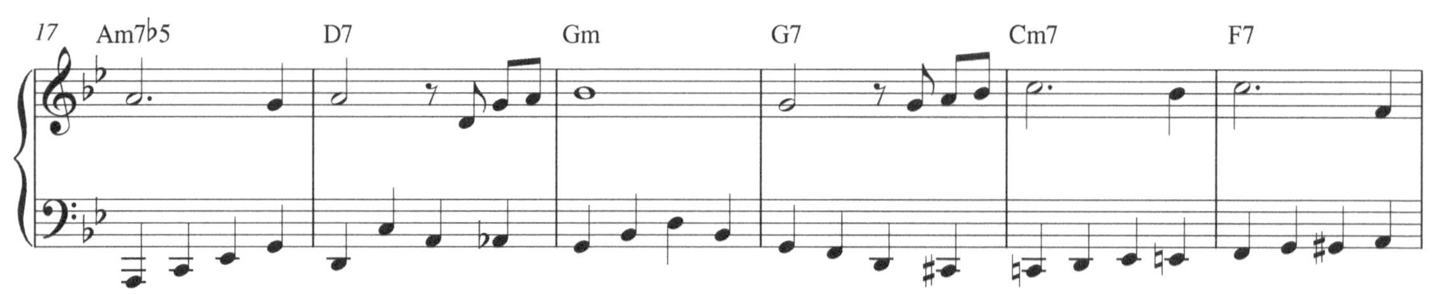

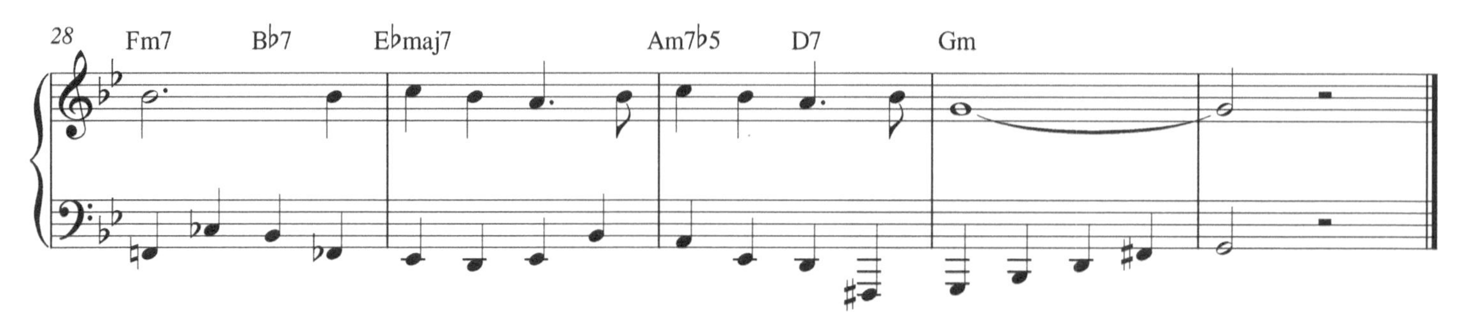

"Nothin' Changes"

So-called "rhythm changes" is a term used for the chord changes to George and Ira Gershwin's "I Got Rhythm." Many jazz songs, especially bebop tunes, are based on that chord progression.

"Nothin' Changes" uses "rhythm changes" as its model and is shown with a half-note bass line. A majority of the chords are of half-note duration, allowing for mostly root motions. The bridge, by contrast, contains two-measure chord lengths, which allows for more possibilities.

Track 20

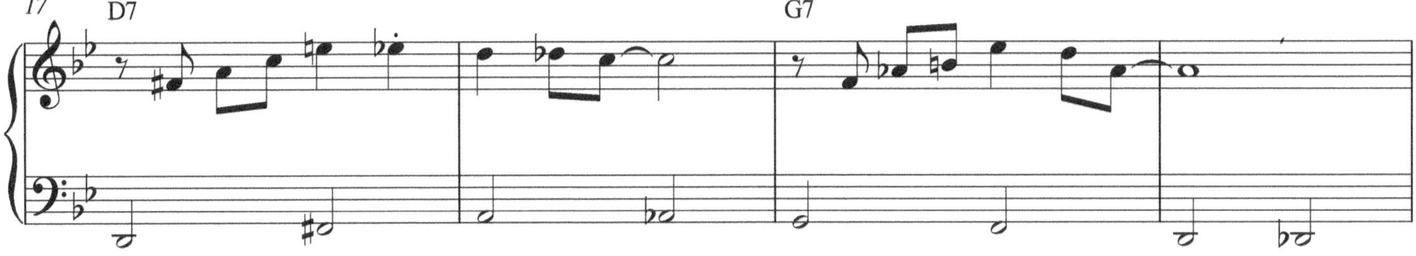

When chord durations last for two or more measures, a half-note bass line can be treated like a walking bass line with stepwise motions that include passing and neighbor tones. This example is for the bridge of "Nothin' Changes."

"Nothin' Changes" with Walking Bass

Here is a walking bass line for "rhythm changes."

Track 22

MELODY, BASS, AND CHORDS

"St. Louis Blues"

What follows is a step-by-step approach to playing a tune with melody and chords in the right hand while playing a walking bass line in the left hand. We'll use the first section of W.C. Handy's "St. Louis Blues" as our example.

1. Play the melody with a simple half-note bass line.

Track 23

2. Play the melody in the right hand while building chords below as the harmony changes. The notes chosen will depend on the nature of the melody in regard to facilitation. The root usually is not necessary as the bass will most likely play it. The fifth is also expendable in favor of the third, seventh, and extended tones.

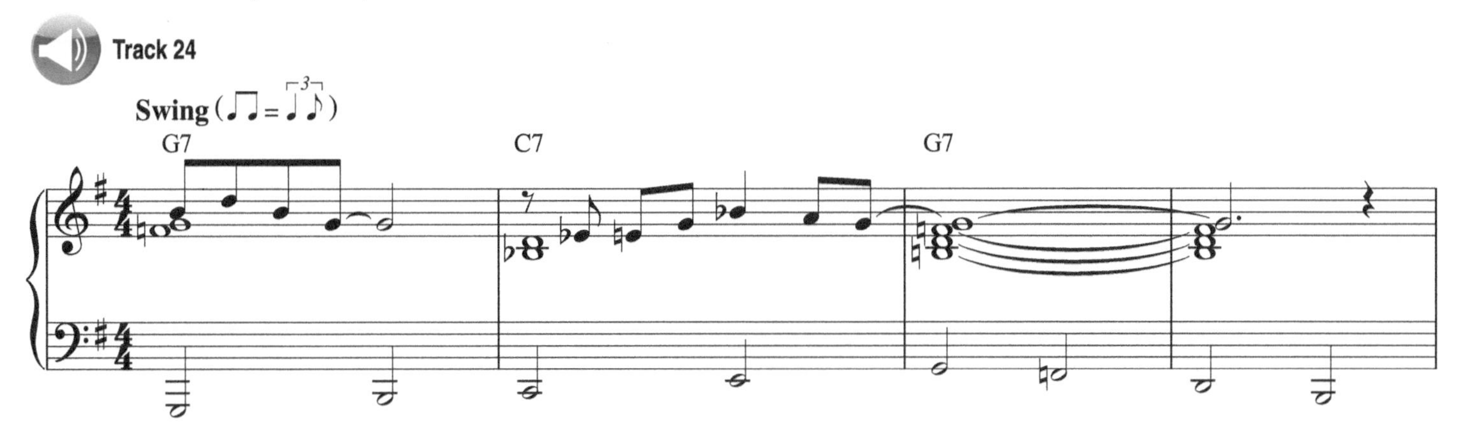

3. Activate the chords rhythmically by comping and creating motion when possible – to fill in those places where the melody is inactive.

4. Play the melody along with a walking bass line.

5. Play the melody while comping chords in the right hand (as in step 3) with a walking bass line.

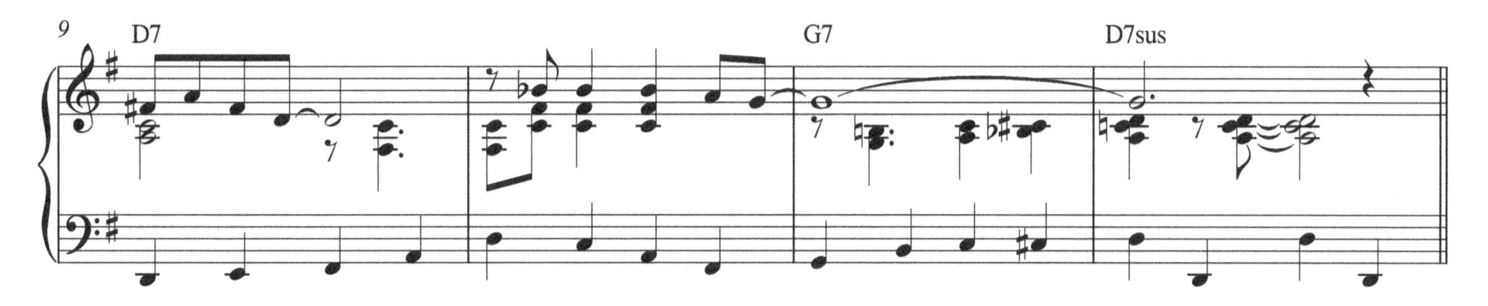

"Rose Room"

"Rose Room" is a standard that served as a model for Duke Ellington's "In a Mellow Tone." The melody with a sample walking bass line is shown in the next example.

9
G♭7
A♭maj7
G♭7
F7

13
B♭7
E♭7
F7

17
B♭7
E♭7
A♭maj7
A♭6

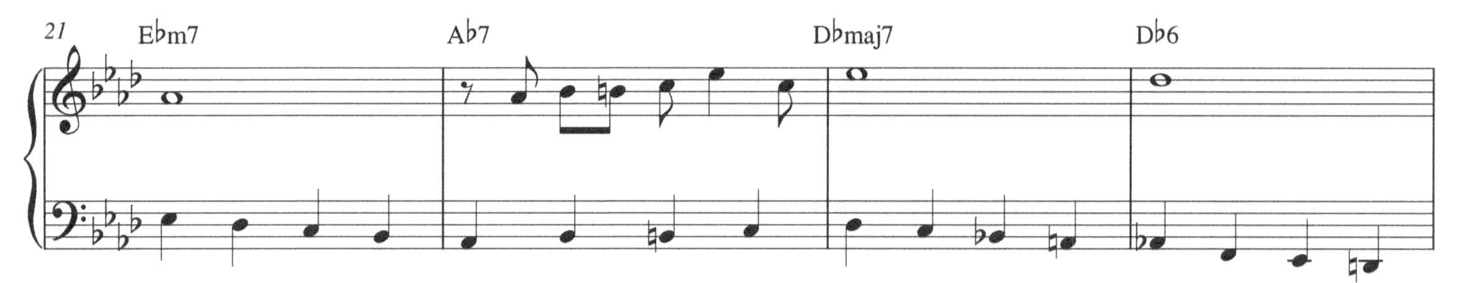
21
E♭m7
A♭7
D♭maj7
D♭6

25
G♭7
A♭maj7
G♭7
F7

29
B♭7
E♭7
A♭6

Play a swing version of "Rose Room" with a walking bass while comping chords in the right hand, as demonstrated below.

CHAPTER 4
HARMONIC EMBELLISHMENT

When we encounter an inactive chord progression, there are several ways to create harmonic movement and interest. These procedures can be useful for solo playing in the absence of a rhythm section. A few common devices are shown below. (For a thorough description of these techniques, see my books *Intros, Endings, and Turnarounds* and *Bebop Jazz Piano*, published by Hal Leonard Corporation.)

DIATONIC STEPWISE PROLONGATION

A static harmony can be prolonged by diatonic movement away from and back to the original chord. In the following example, the original inert A♭ harmony is replaced with a diatonic stepwise progression that gives motion to the music.

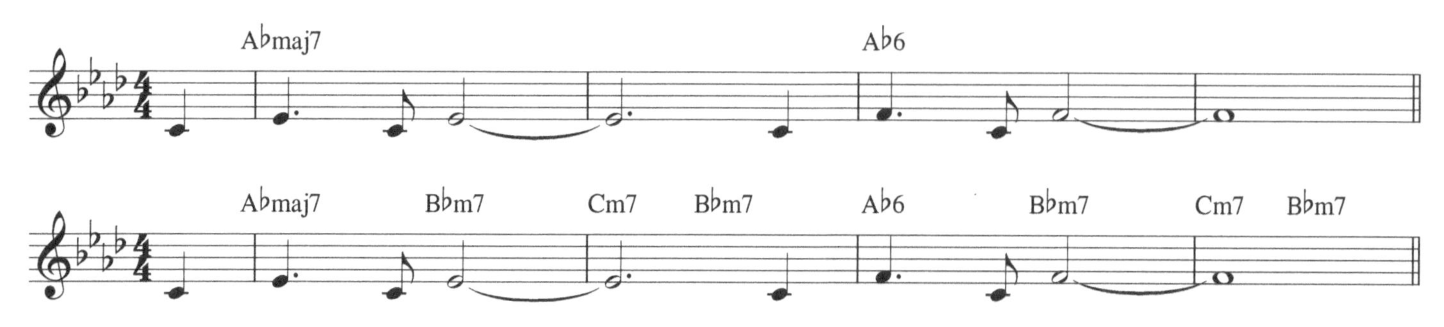

MOVEMENT WITHIN A CHORD

When a chord lasts for a measure or more, simple stepwise movement within the chord can create motion. Stepwise chords from root position to the first inversion of the chord are often played with chords built from a stepwise bass line. Compare the written bridge for "Nothin' Changes" (see page 35) with the re-harmonized version below. (Enharmonic adjustments have been made to facilitate reading.) In a circle of descending fifths (ascending fourths) progressions, these motions can continue the stepwise bass movement.

DOMINANT INFLECTION

Motion can be created for stationary chords by inflecting them with the dominant chord. For example, a Dm7 can move to an A7 and back again without disrupting the harmonic flow of the music. The second example below shows a dominant inflection of the E♭m7 chord as well as a prolongation of the D♭maj7 chord.

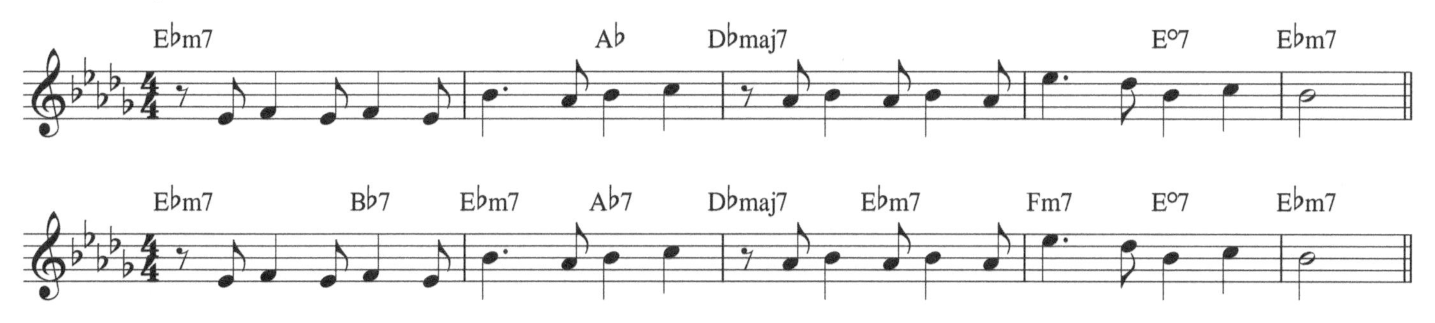

HARMONIC DISPLACEMENT

Sometimes chords are displaced by others that can add motion to – but do not disrupt – the harmonic direction and goals. In the example below, a I-V progression in C major is turned into a I-vi-ii-V progression by displacing the C6 for an Am7 and placing the Dm7 before the G7.

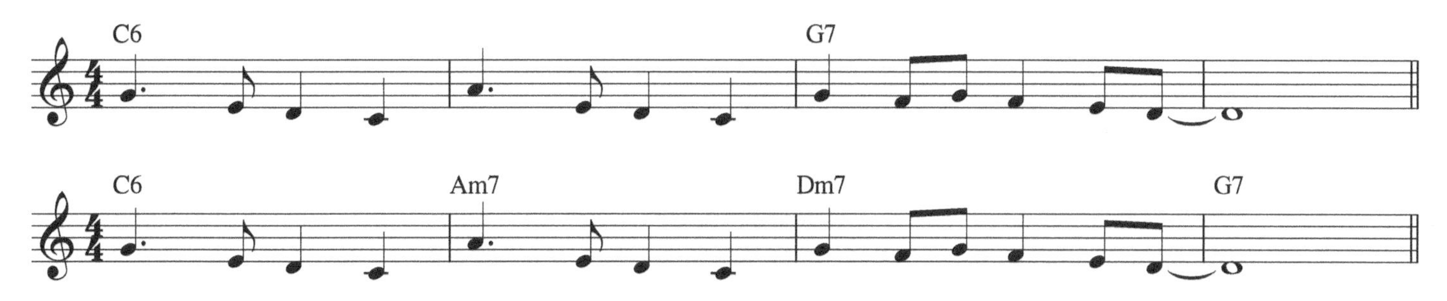

PASSING CHORDS

Often, chords are inserted between harmonies a step apart. In the following example, a Dm7 is placed between the Cmaj7 and Em7 and a B♭7 is placed between the Cmaj7 and A7 in the last measure.

NEIGHBOR CHORDS

Motion can be added to a fixed chord by moving up or down a step and back to the original chord.

APPOGGIATURA CHORDS

A chord can be approached by a chord a half step above. This gives a leaning motion to the target chord in much the same way that leading tones do in a bass line.

HARMONIC SUBSTITUTION

Tunes are frequently re-harmonized using substitute chords. In the second example below, the Cmaj7 is replaced with an Em7 in the third measure. This kind of substitution delays a resolution to the tonic and often is used for turnarounds at the ends of tunes or sections.

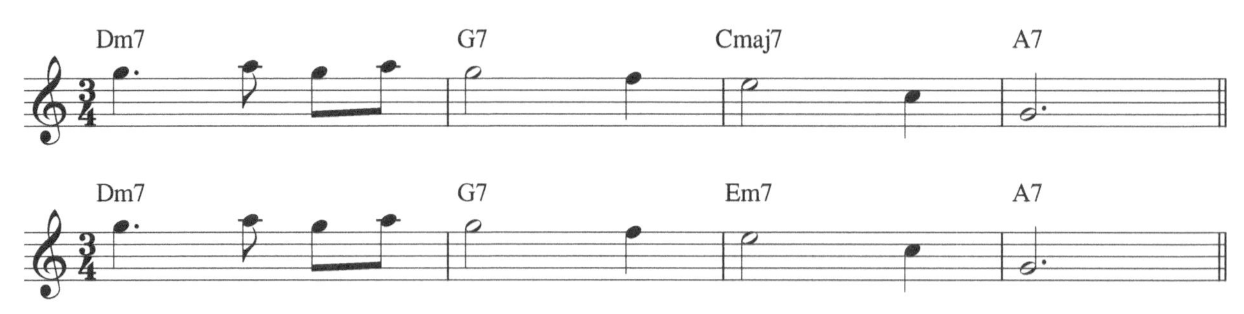

Tritone substitution is a standard practice used in jazz. It almost always works for dominant seventh chords a tritone apart, but can used in other ways as well. In typical descending Circle of Fifths progressions, this changes the root motion from down a fifth to down a half step. This is often technically convenient, especially for a solo pianist. In the next example, the movement by descending fifths of the Em7–A7♭9–Dm7–G7♭9 is turned into the descending chromatic movement of Em7–E♭m7–Dm7–D♭7 through tritone substitution. Passing chords are also used.

LINEAR MOTION

Stepwise lines within a chord can create motion without fundamentally changing the harmony. The following example shows this type of motion for an otherwise static Em7 chord. Here, the linear motion traverses the notes E-D♯-D-C♯ and can be placed in any voice.

The next example contains a rising linear motion beginning on the note A, the fifth of the D minor chord.

PEDAL TONES

Pedal tones are held (or repeated) notes that remain constant even though the harmony changes. While pedal tones create an immobile voice within the harmonic flow, they actually cause a sense of motion because of the tension they produce and the release thereafter. Pedal tones also give the pianist a momentary respite from constant left-hand movement. Most pedal tones are played on the dominant or tonic of the prevailing key. The following example, from the second half of "Winter Comes," uses a dominant pedal on the note D in the key of G minor.

The examples in this chapter only scratch the surface of re-harmonization techniques, but they should serve to get you thinking in these terms and interested in exploring this topic further.

"WHEN YOU AND I WERE YOUNG, MAGGIE"

Below is a basic lead sheet of "When You and I Were Young, Maggie," an old favorite from the 19th century. The arrangement that follows the lead sheet makes use of the re-harmonization techniques demonstrated in this chapter.

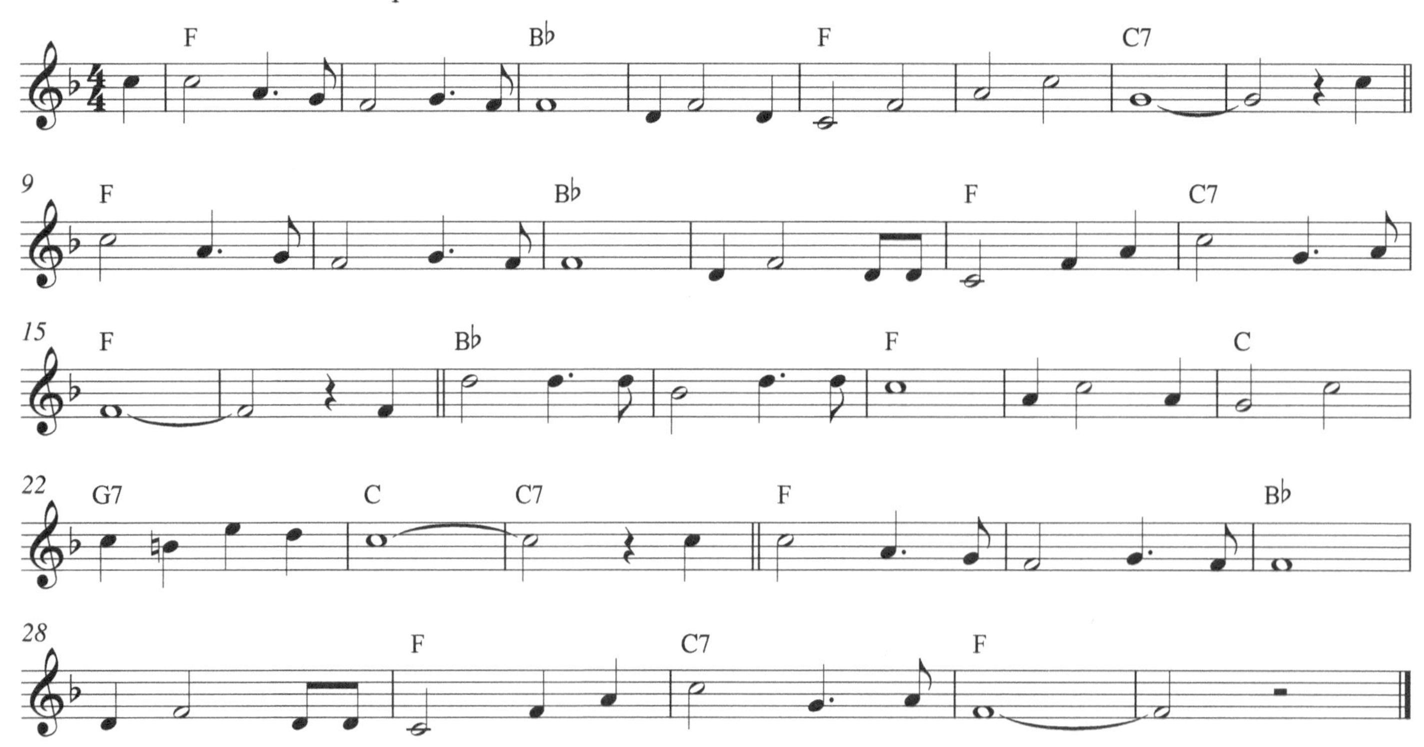

When You and I Were Young, Maggie

Track 32

Words by George W. Johnson
Music by James Austin Butterfield

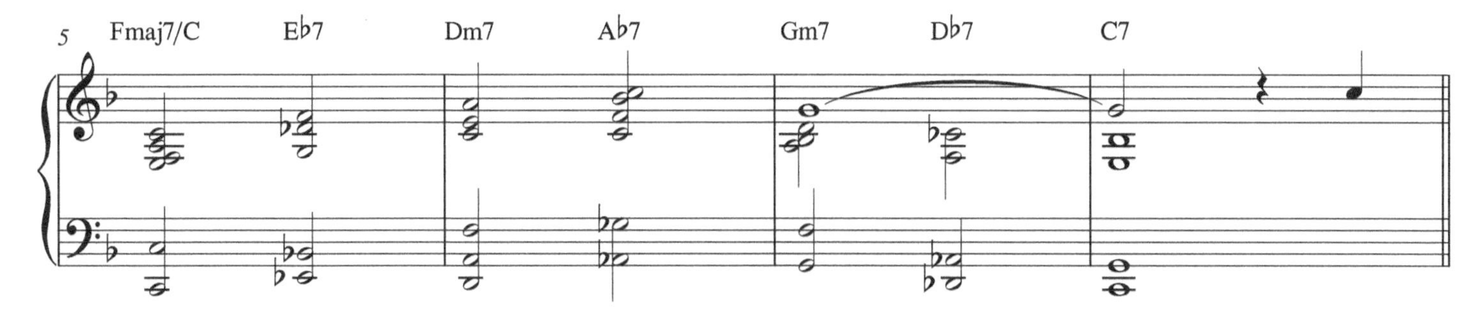

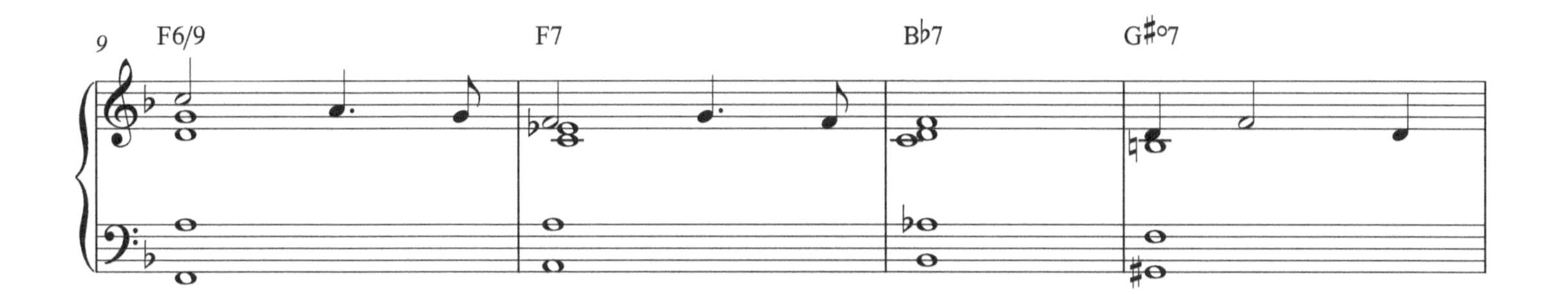

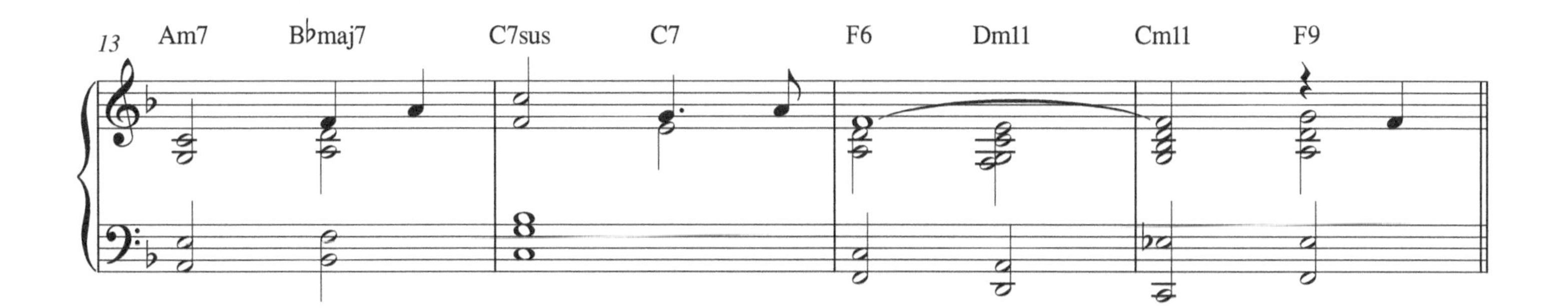

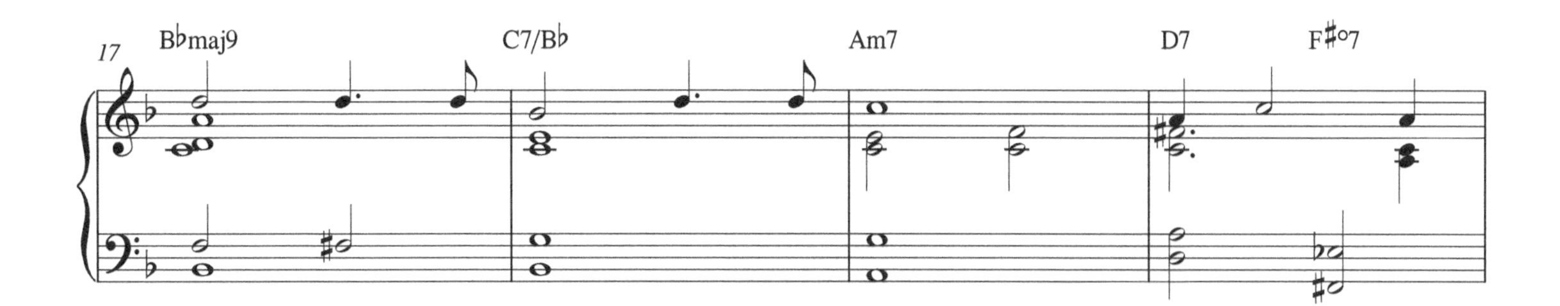

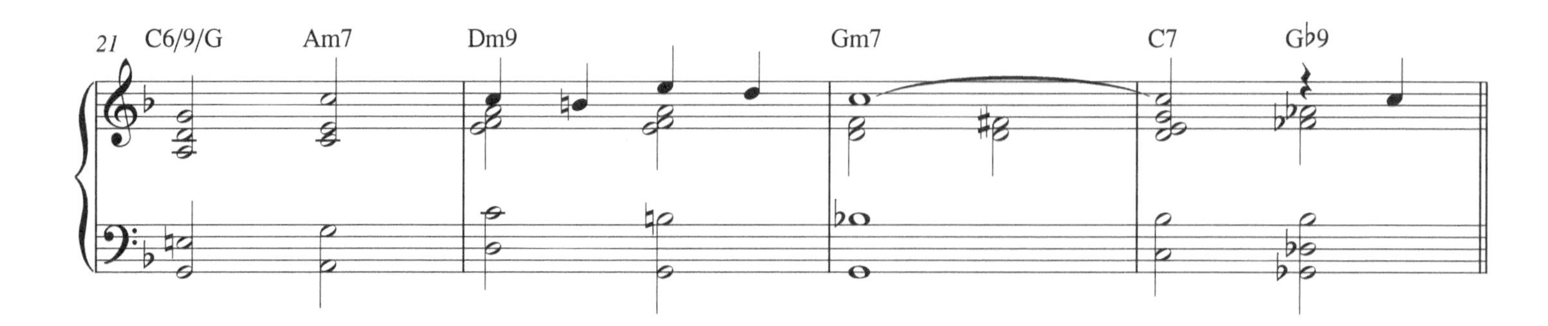
21
C6/9/G
Am7
Dm9
Gm7
C7
G♭9

25
Fmaj9
Gm7
G♯°7
F7/A
B♭maj9
Bm7♭5
E7

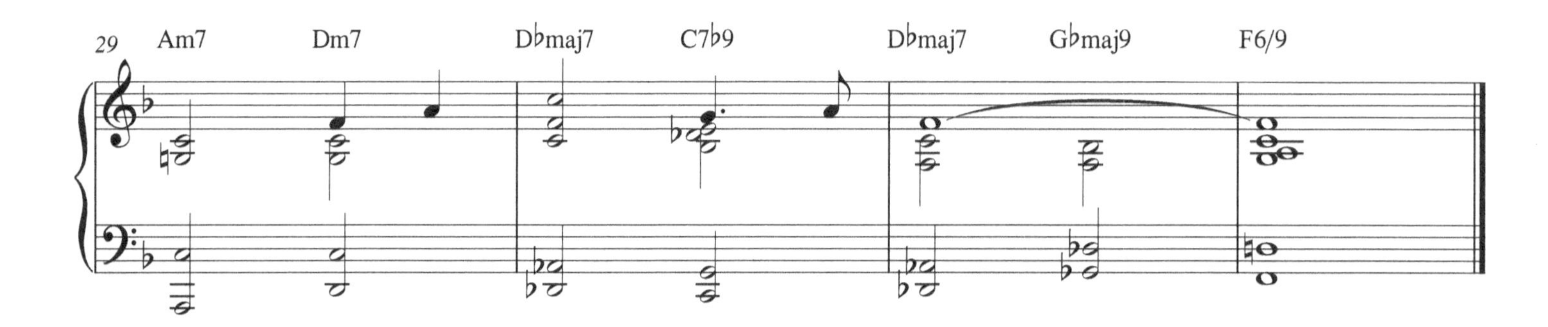
29
Am7
Dm7
D♭maj7
C7♭9
D♭maj7
G♭maj9
F6/9

CHAPTER 5
SWING TUNES

This chapter demonstrates a step-by-step approach to playing tunes with a swing feel.

INDIANA

"Indiana (Back Home Again in Indiana)" is a jazz standard that dates back to 1917. Its chord progression has served as a basis for several other tunes, including "Donna Lee" and "Ju-Ju." "Indiana" will serve as an example of how to dissect a swing tune and reassemble it for a solo piano performance. The lead sheet is on page 96.

Melody and Root Bass

Play "Indiana" with a single-note melody and simple root bass part, as follows.

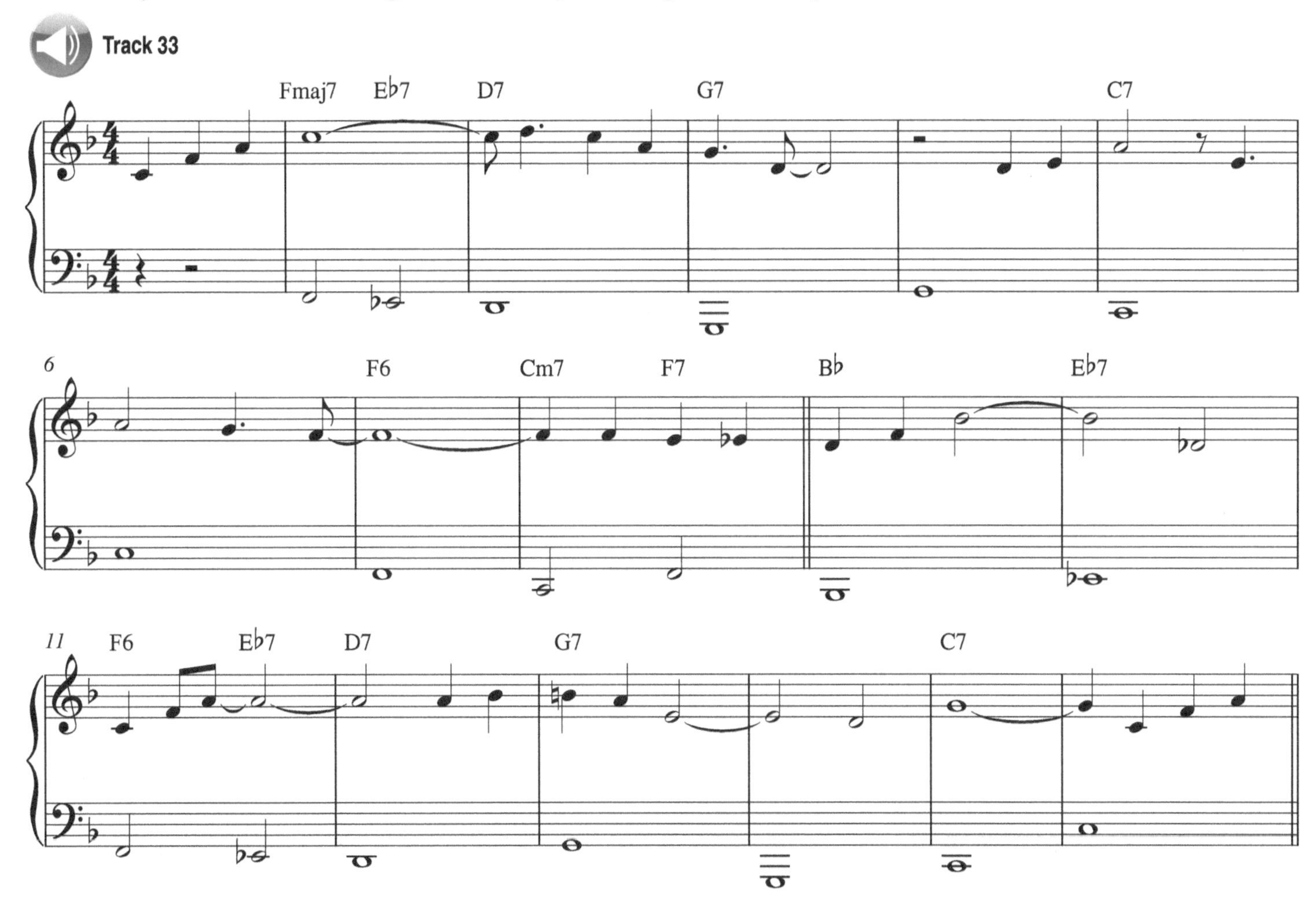

Melody and Simple Left-Hand Chords

Next, play "Indiana" with a single-note melody and left-hand chords. Keep the chords simple, with four-note voicings using inversions, to facilitate smooth voice leading.

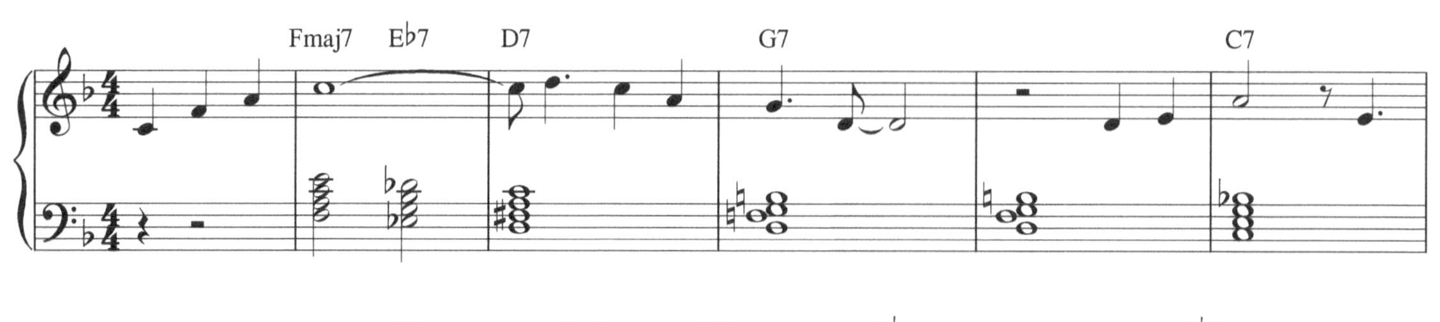

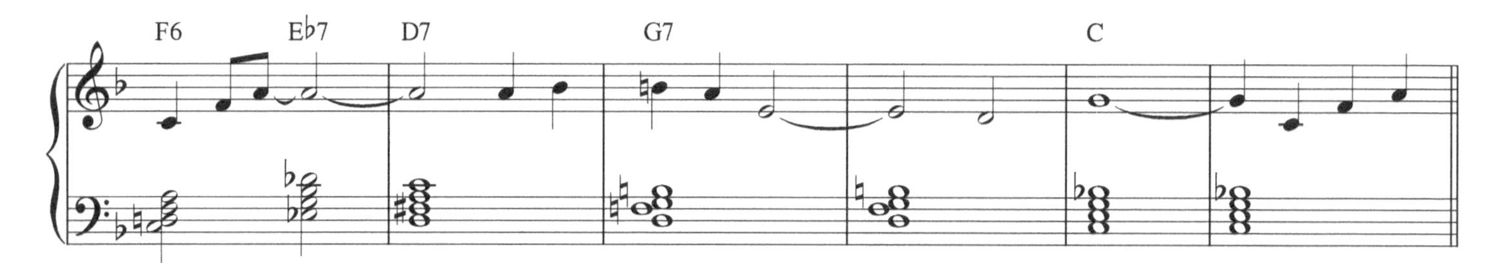

Melody with Left-Hand Comping

Comp chords in a swing feel using two- or three-note voicings

Melody and Rootless Voicings in the Left Hand

Comp chords in a similar way with rootless voicings.

Track 35

Swing

Fmaj7 E♭7 D7 G7

5 Gm7 C7 F6 Cm7 F7

Open-Chord Voicings with Two Hands

Play through the chords of "Indiana" with open voicing with both hands. Experiment with different ways of voicing the chords that connect them smoothly. Below is one of many possibilities using five-note open voicings.

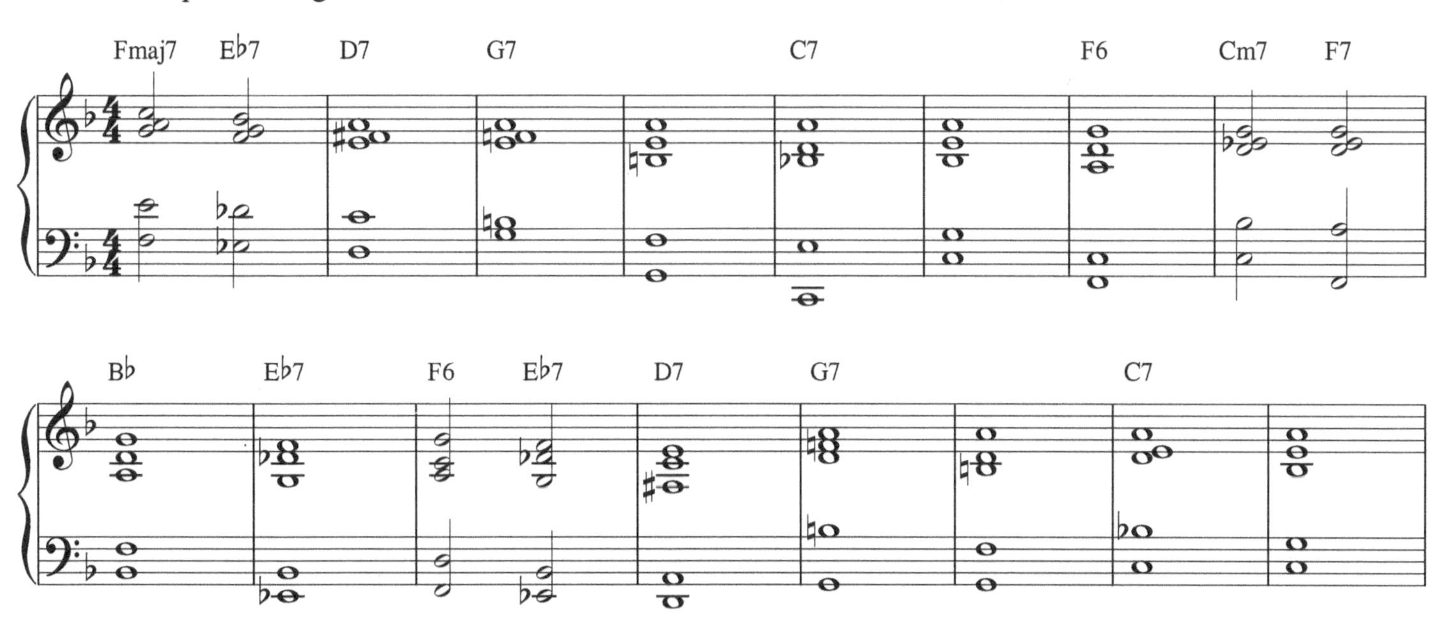

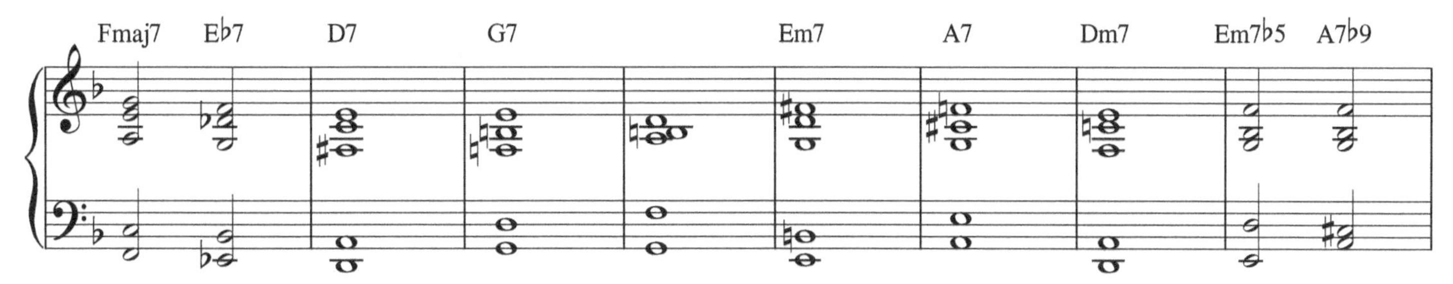

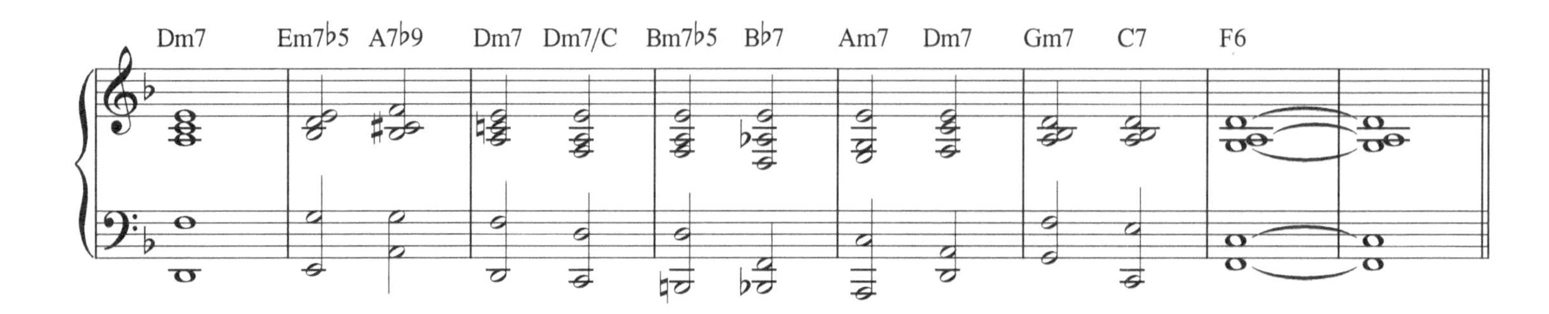

Melody and Open Chords with Both Hands

Next, play the tune with full open voicing in both hands. There are many ways to do this, so try several alternatives. You will discover certain voicings work better than others, depending on where the register of the melody lies in relation to the chords. One potential realization follows.

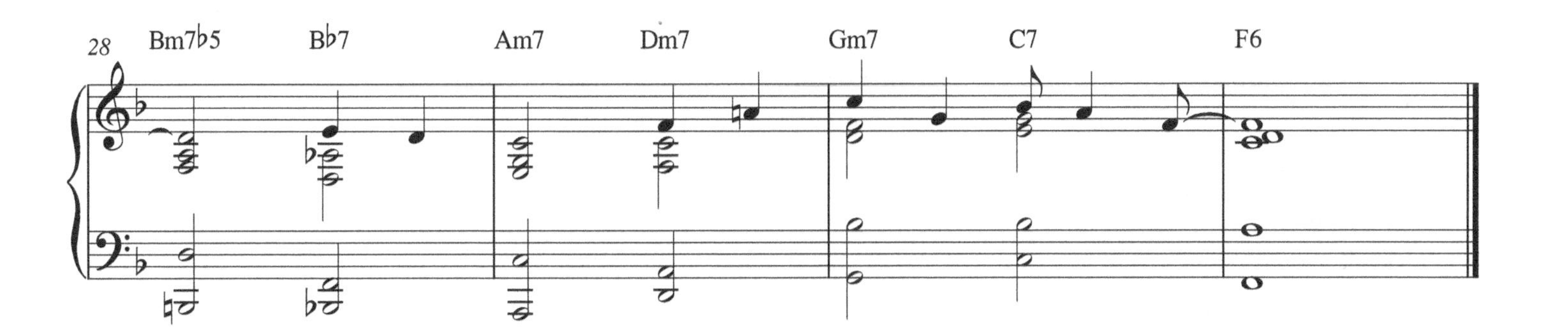

Open-Voicing Comping

Play through "Indiana" comping open-voicing chords while singing the melody aloud or in your head.

Track 36

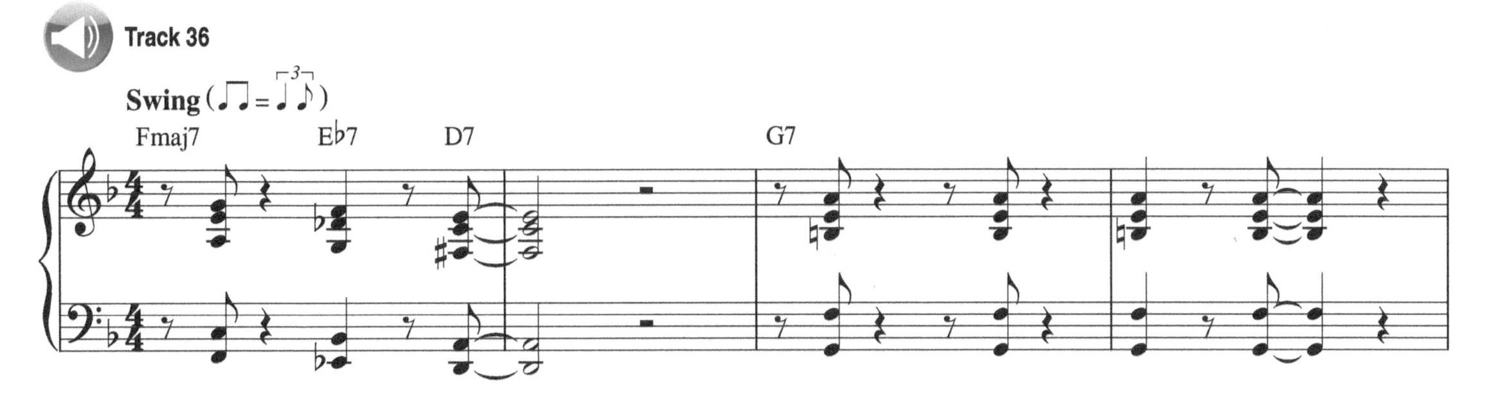

Melody with Open-Voicing Comping

Play "Indiana" with a swing feel using open voicings.

Track 37

Melody with Half-Note Bass Line

Play "Indiana" in a swing style using a half-note bass line in the left hand. There are many ways to do this. (Refer to Chapter 3.) This example gives but one option.

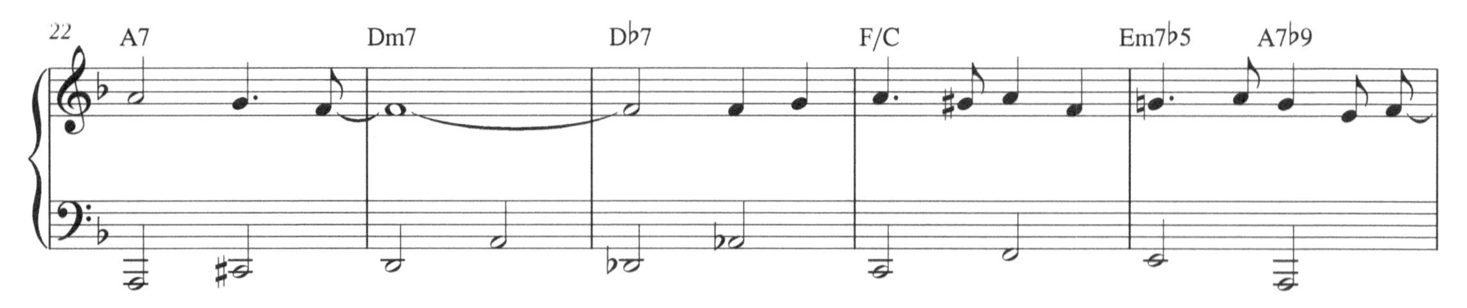

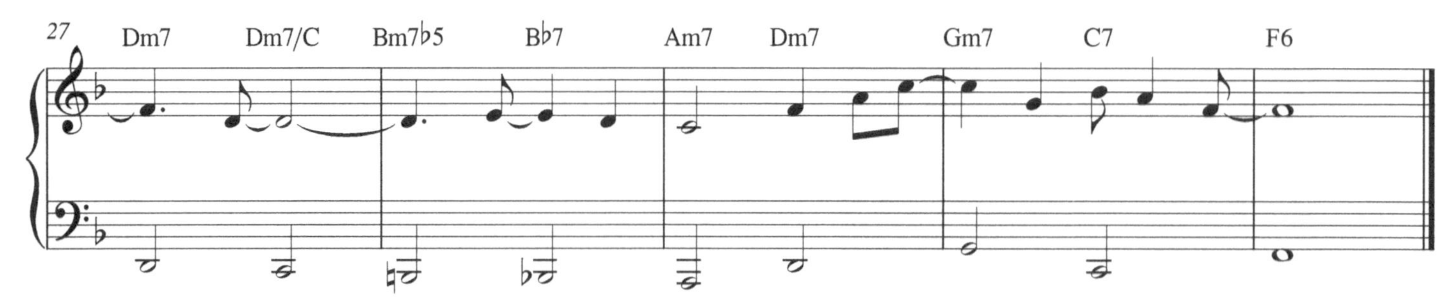

Melody with Bass and Guide Tones in the Left Hand

Play the melody with bass notes and guide tones, either at the same time or displaced.

Track 39

Melody with Walking Bass Line

Try a walking bass line along with a single-note melody. One possibility follows. Try others.

Track 40

12
D7
G7
C7

16
Fmaj7
E♭7
D7
G7

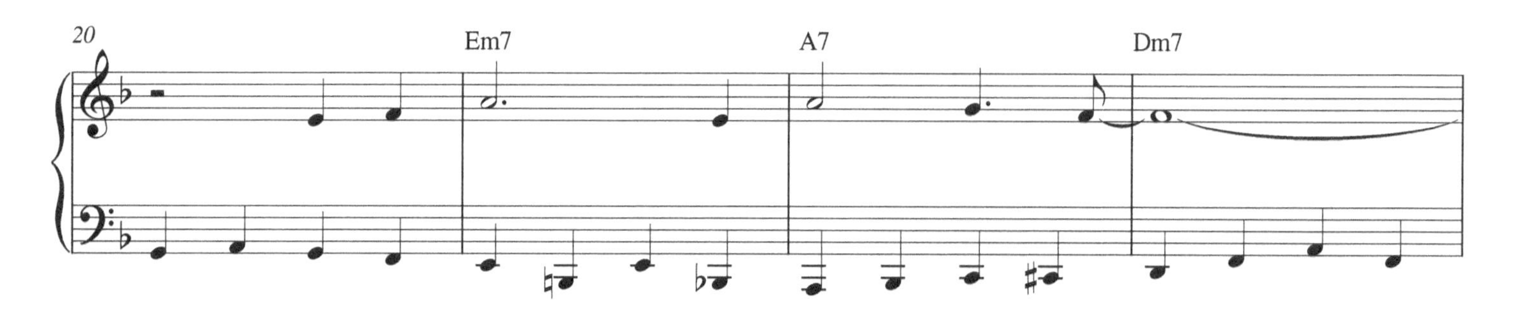
20
Em7
A7
Dm7

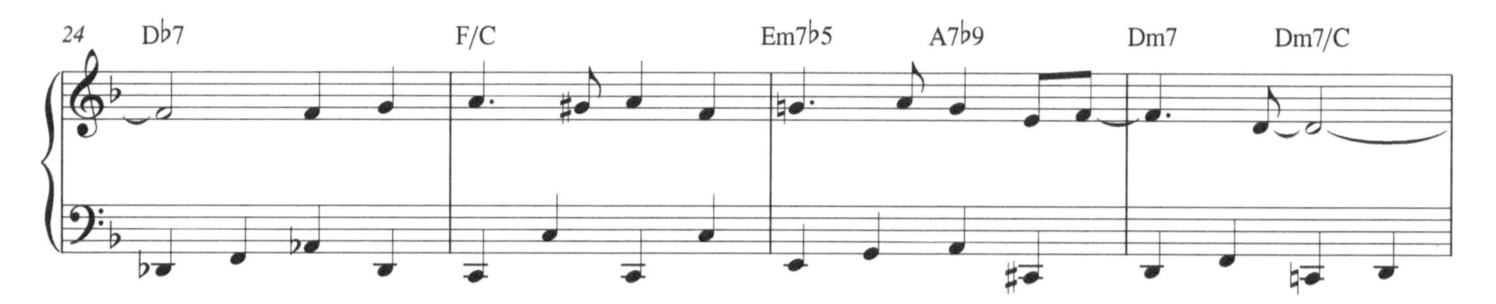
24
D♭7
F/C
Em7♭5
A7♭9
Dm7
Dm7/C

28
Bm7♭5
B♭7
Am7
Dm7
Gm7
C7
F6

Melody and Comping with Walking Bass

Comp right-hand chords along with melody and walking bass.

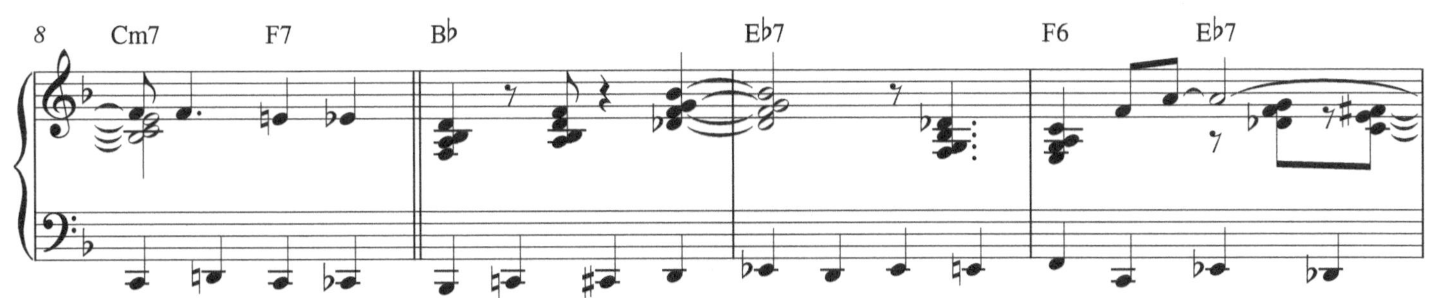

Combined Solo Arrangement

The following arrangement combines most of the techniques described above, as well as re-harmonization for added motion. After learning it, try to create your own arrangement and practice improvising new ones.

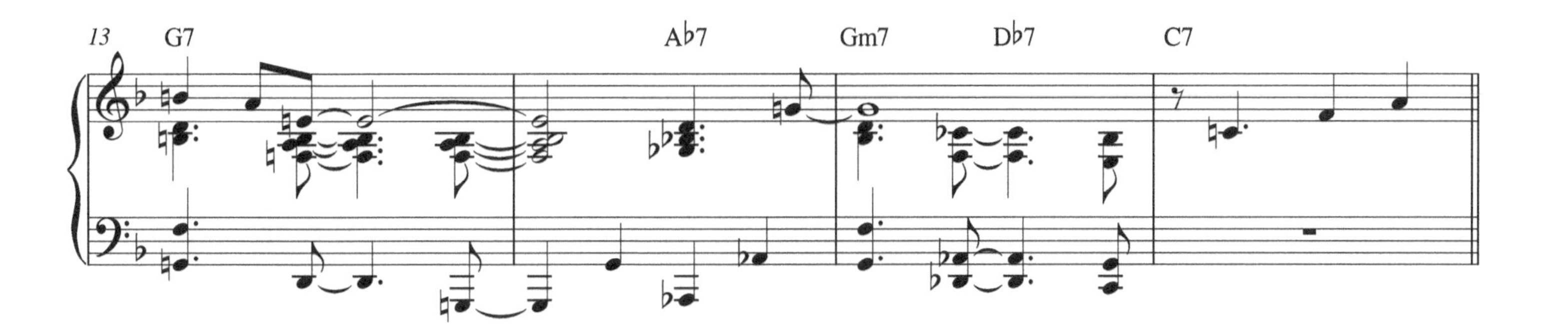
13
G7
A♭7
Gm7
D♭7
C7

17
F9
E9
E♭9
D9
D7
G7
A♭7
G7

21
Em7
A7
Dm7
D♭7

25
F/C
Em7♭5
A7♭9
Dm7
Dm7/C
Bm7♭5
B♭7

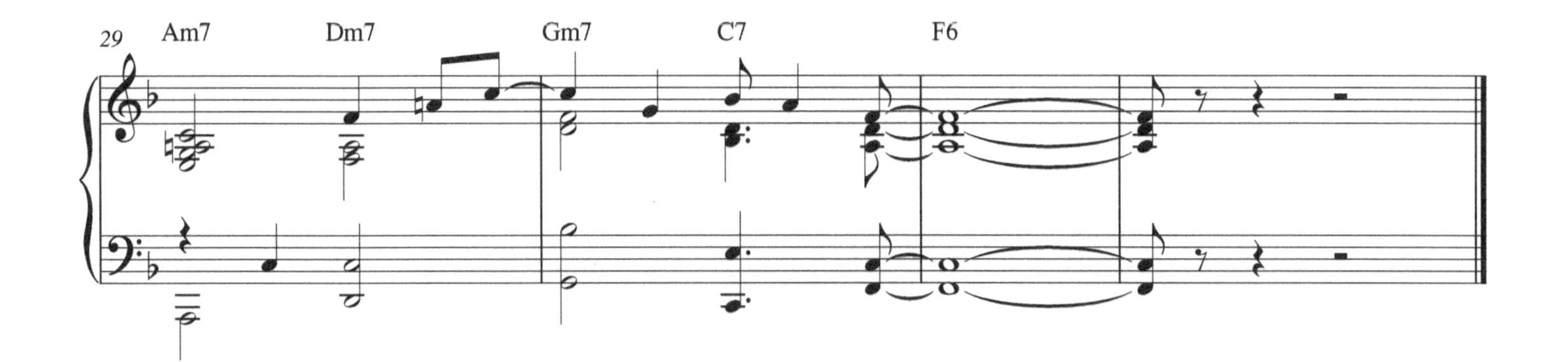
29
Am7
Dm7
Gm7
C7
F6

"POOR BUTTERFLY"

"Poor Butterfly" is another old standard that jazz musicians have played for many years. The lead sheet is on page 97. Go through the same steps outlined for "Indiana" before proceeding to the examples below.

Melody with Open Voicings

After playing through this example, perform it again while activating the right- and left-hand rhythms to make it swing – as shown above for "Indiana."

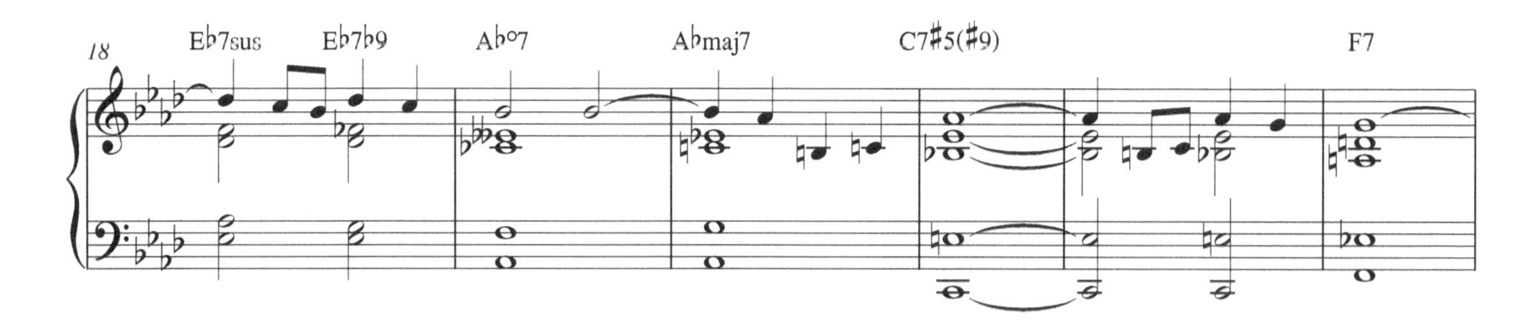

Melody with Half-Note Bass

The bass line used here makes use of some of the advanced techniques described in Chapter 3.

Track 44

Melody with Walking Bass

Track 45

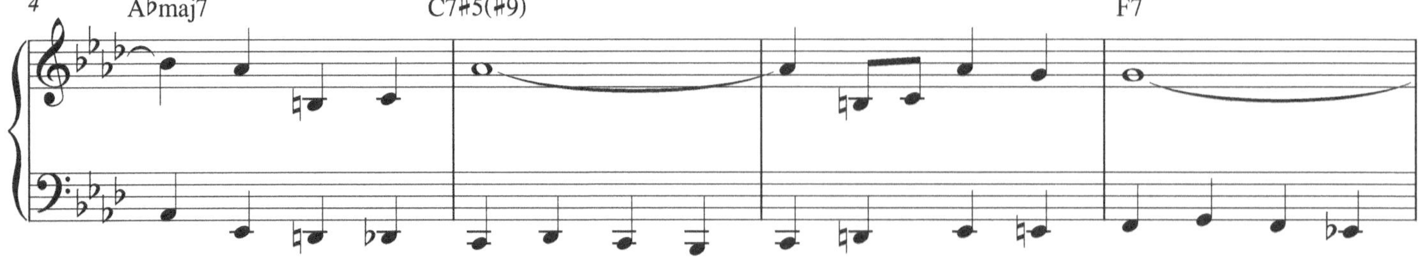

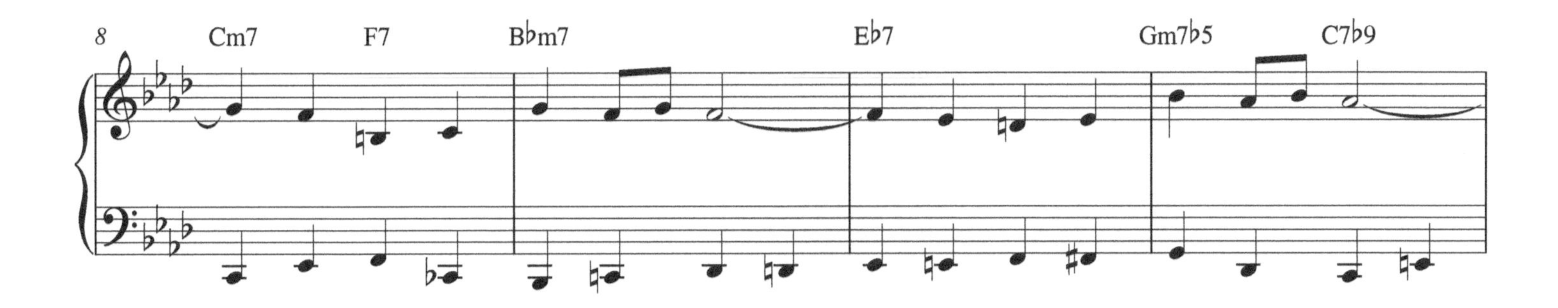
8
Cm7
F7
B♭m7
E♭7
Gm7♭5
C7♭9

12
Fm7
B♭7
E♭7sus

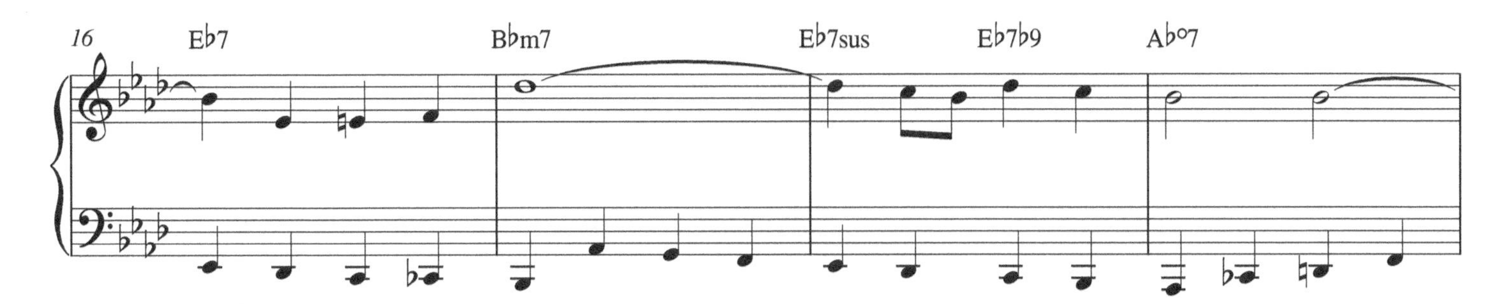
16
E♭7
B♭m7
E♭7sus
E♭7♭9
A♭°7

20
A♭maj7
C7♯5(♯9)
F7

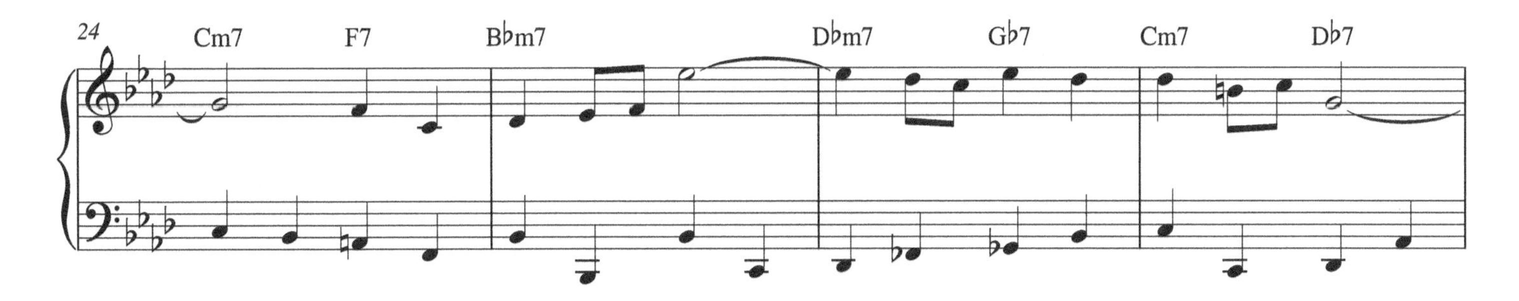
24
Cm7
F7
B♭m7
D♭m7
G♭7
Cm7
D♭7

28
Cm7
B°7
B♭m7
E♭7
A♭°7
A♭maj7

Combined Solo Arrangement

The following arrangement combines most of the techniques described above, as well as reharmonization for added motion. After learning it, try to create your own arrangement and practice improvising new ones.

Track 46

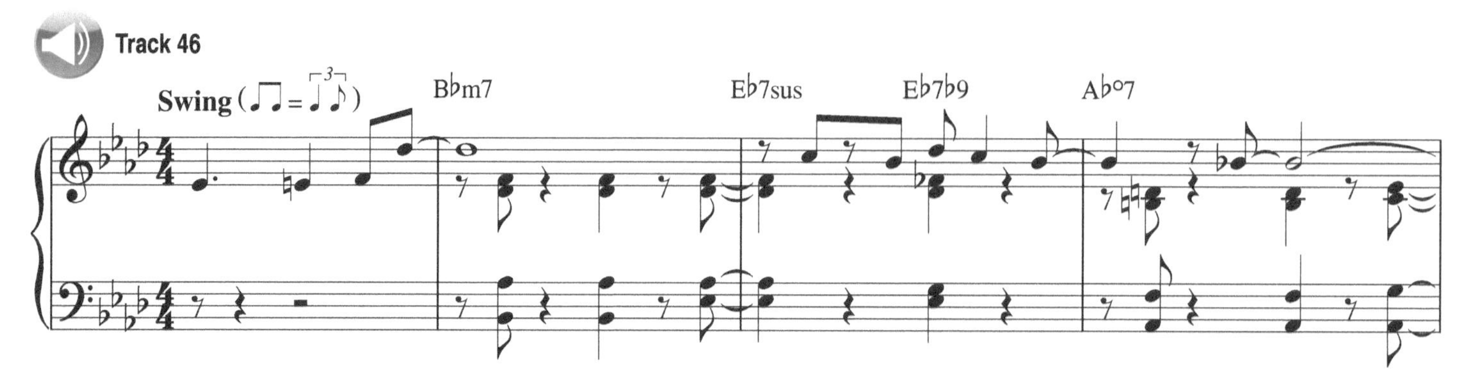

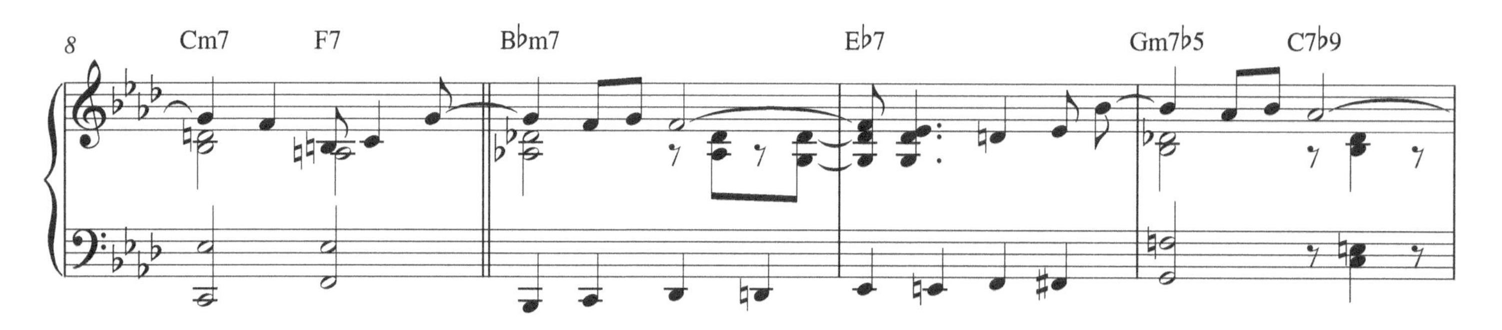

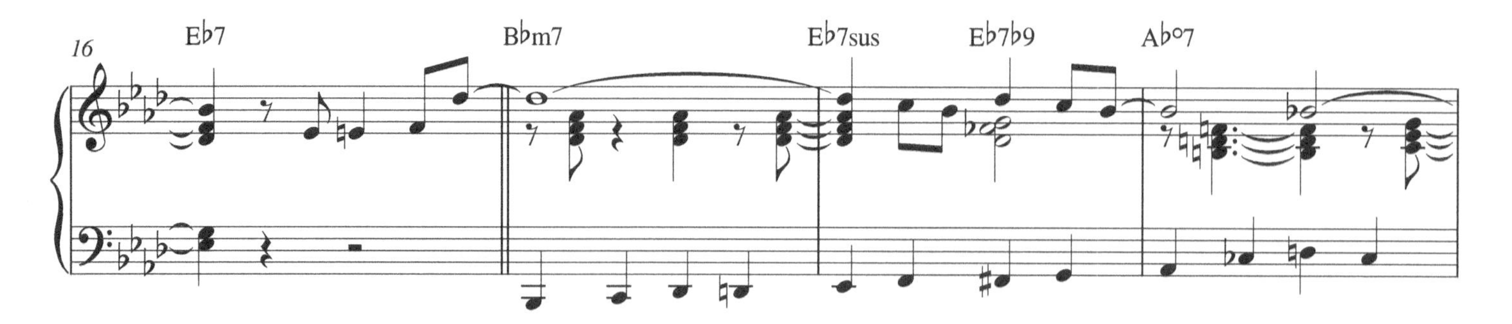

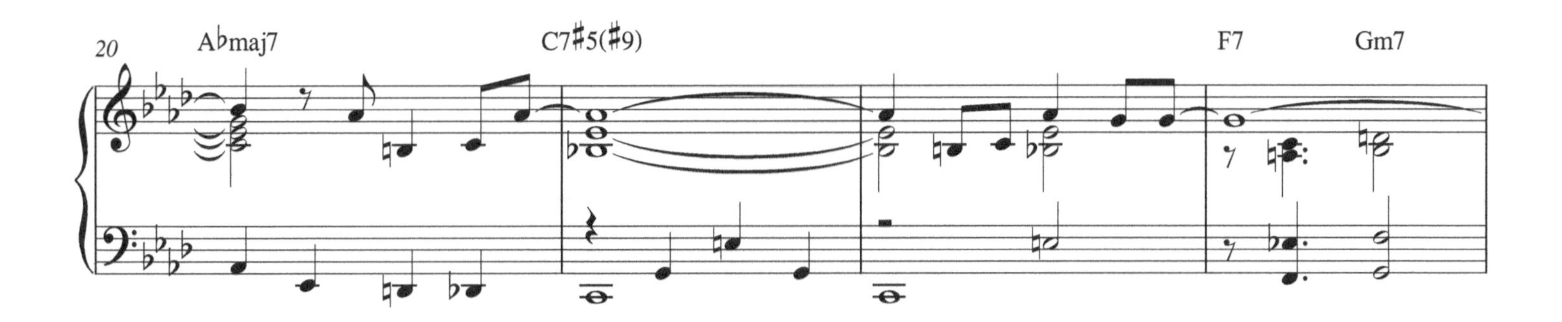

Suggested Swing Tunes to Play

Out of Nowhere

All the Things You Are

Stella by Starlight

Bye, Bye Blackbird

CHAPTER 6
JAZZ WALTZES

Jazz waltzes typically have a lilting quality enabled by a light texture and supple rhythmic accompaniment. While traditional waltz accompaniments contain steady bass-chord-chord quarter notes, jazz waltzes tend to push the chord after the bass note a little ahead of beat 2, as the second part of a swing-eighth note.

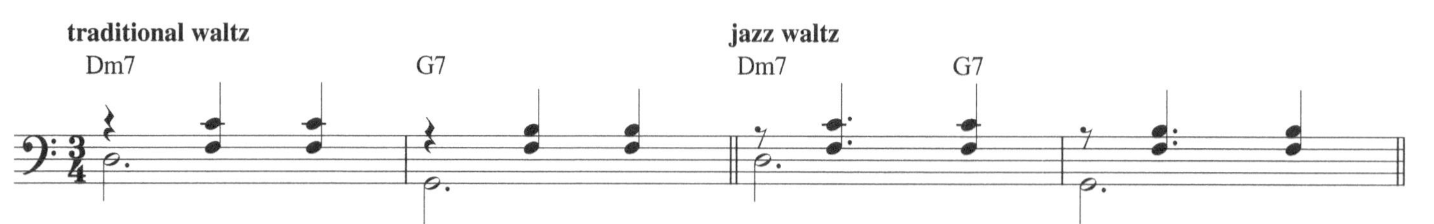

Here are several additional typical jazz waltz accompaniment patterns.

"WENDY'S WALTZ"

An effective solo jazz waltz performance should feature a variety of accompaniment patterns, including the traditional waltz pattern played with several voicings in either or both hands. Suggestions for practicing a jazz waltz are demonstrated below for "Wendy's Waltz." (See the lead sheet on page 99.)

Melody and Bass

As with swing tunes, play the melody with a simple bass part.

Track 47

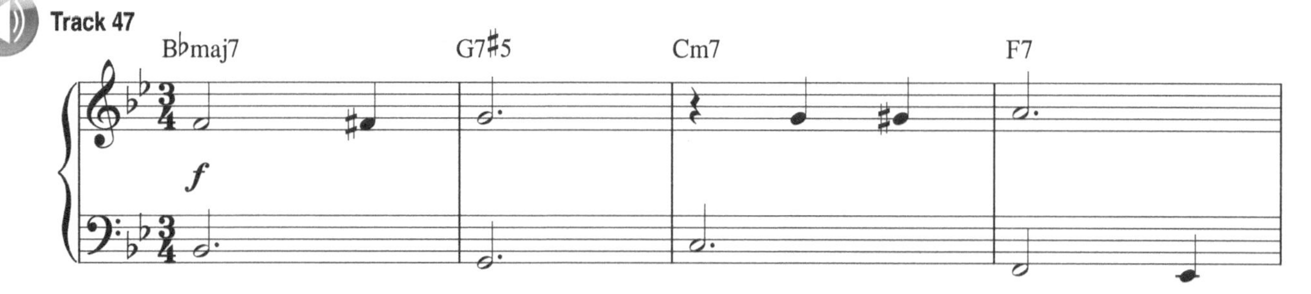

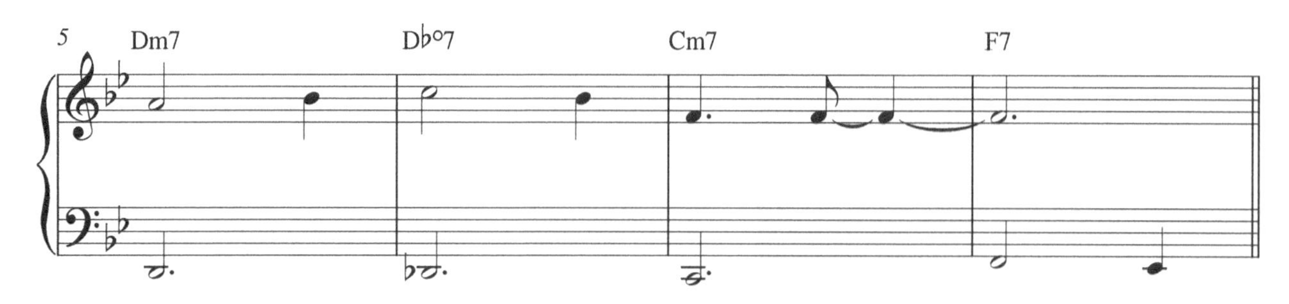

Melody and Simple Left-Hand Jazz Waltz Pattern

Play "Wendy's Waltz" with the simple jazz waltz pattern shown on page 66. Below is an example using bass notes and guide tones. Additionally, play this with each of the other patterns.

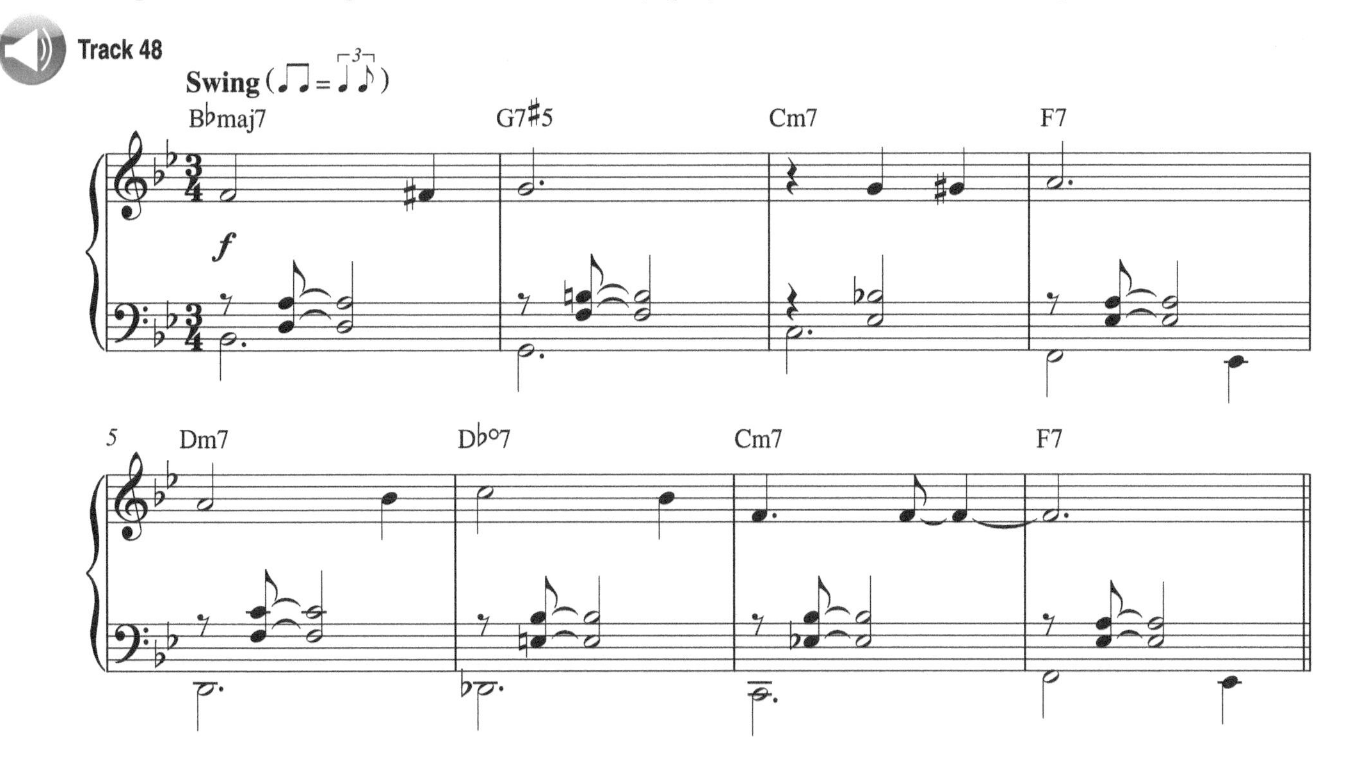

Melody with Mixed Left-Hand Patterns

Play by mixing up the patterns. This can be done in a number of ways; choices often depend on what the right hand is playing, the chords themselves, and the overall desired texture and rhythmic underpinning.

Right-Hand Melody and Chords with Left-Hand Bass

Voice rootless chords below the melody in the right hand.

Track 50

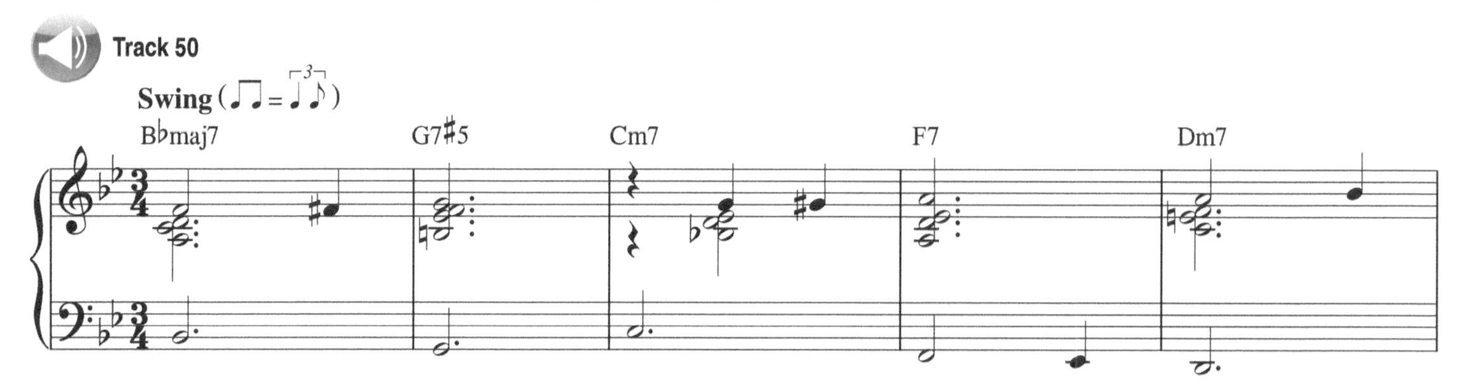

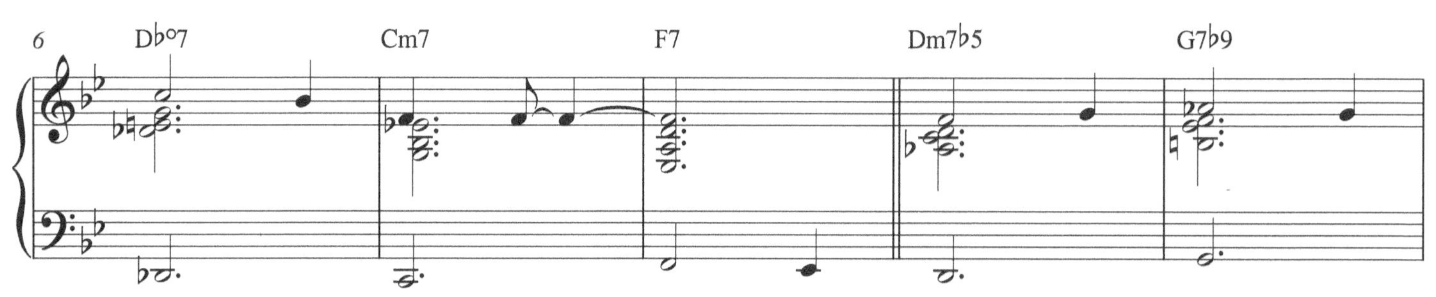

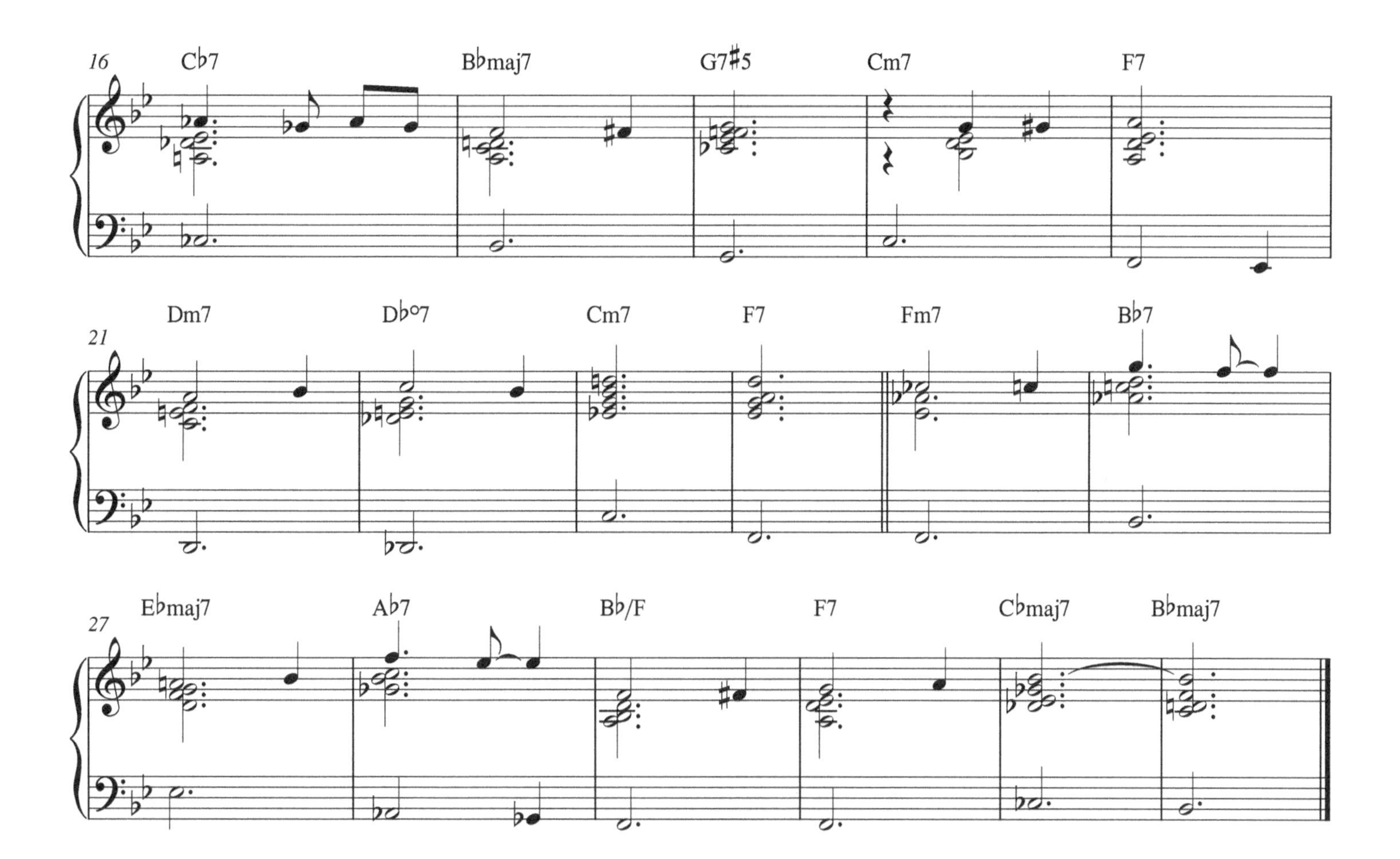

Right-Hand Melody and Comping Chords with Left-Hand Bass

Comp the right-hand chords below the melody using various jazz waltz patterns.

Track 51

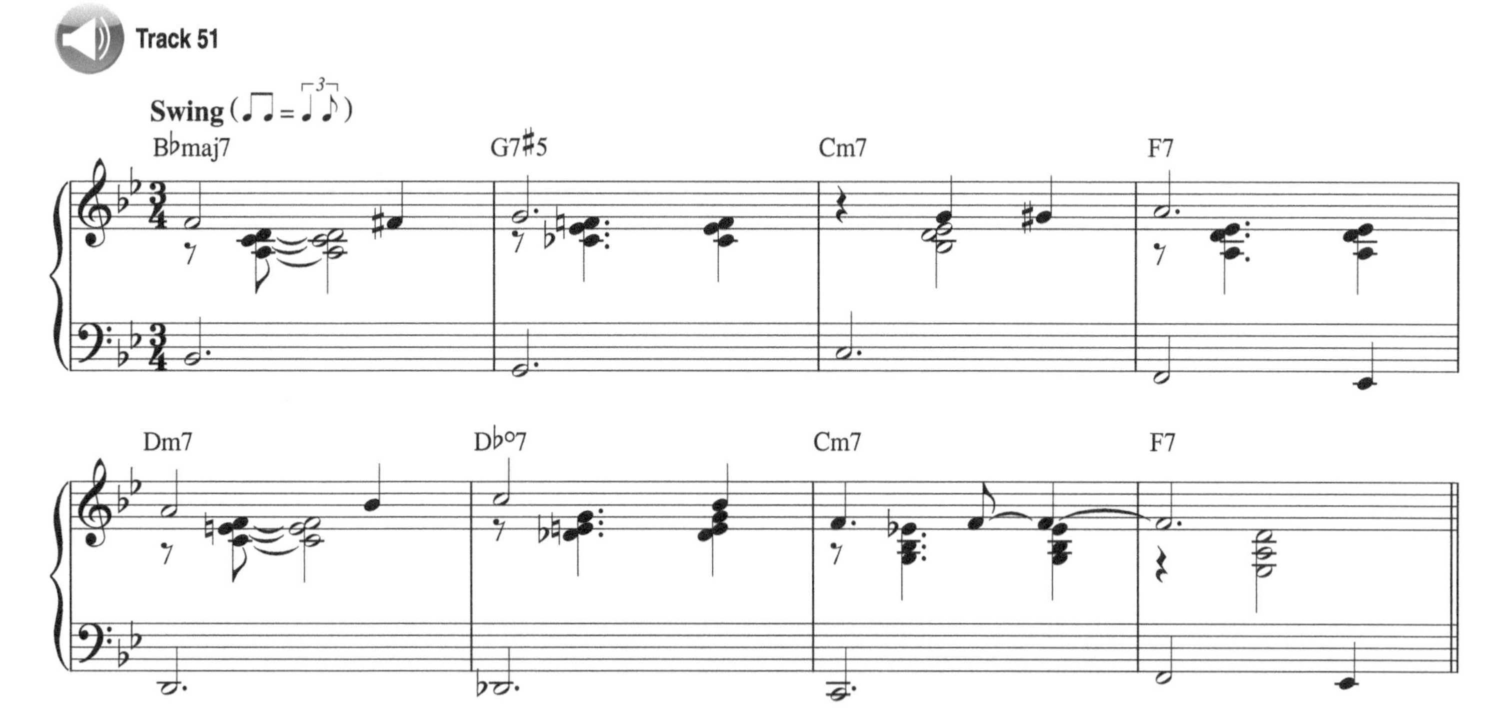

Melody with Open Voicings in Both Hands

This example is one of many ways to play this tune with open voicings.

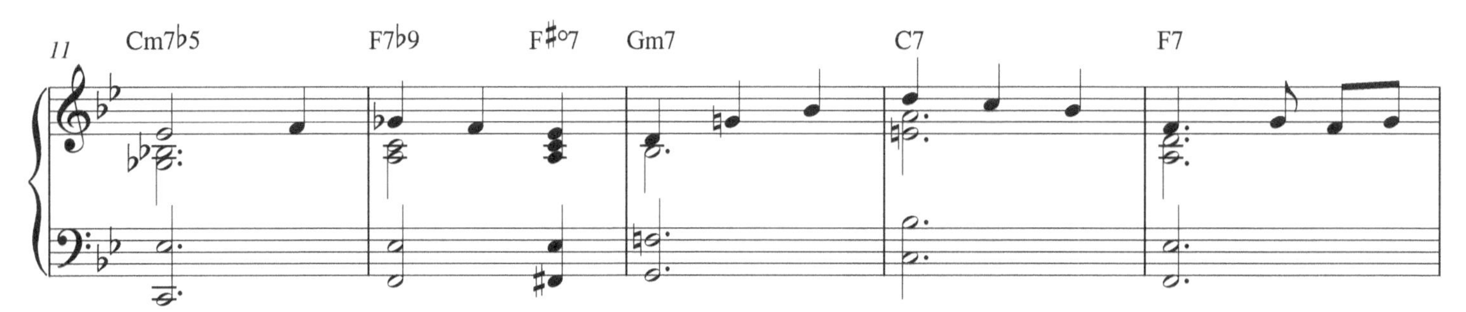

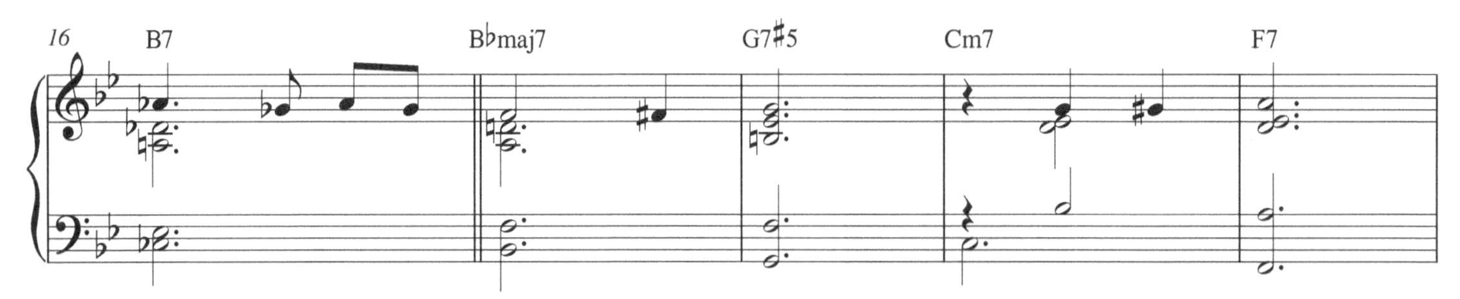

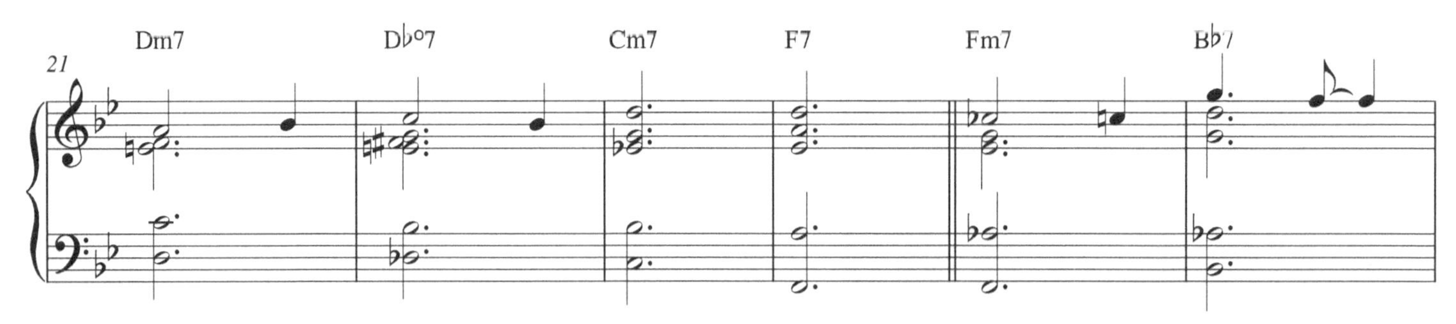

Melody and Comping with Open Voicings

Rhythmically activate the voicings to give a jazz waltz feel.

Track 53

Swing (♫ = ♩♪ triplet)

Bbmaj7 G7#5 Cm7 F7

5 Dm7 Dbo7 Cm7 F7

Combined Solo Arrangement

The following arrangement combines most of the techniques described above. After learning it, create your own arrangement and practice improvising new ones.

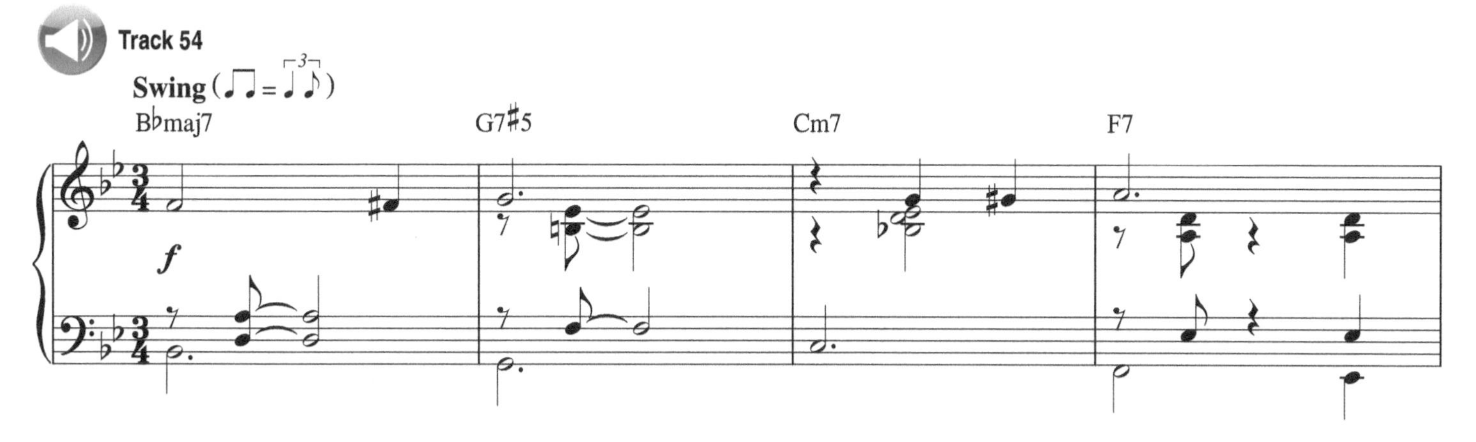

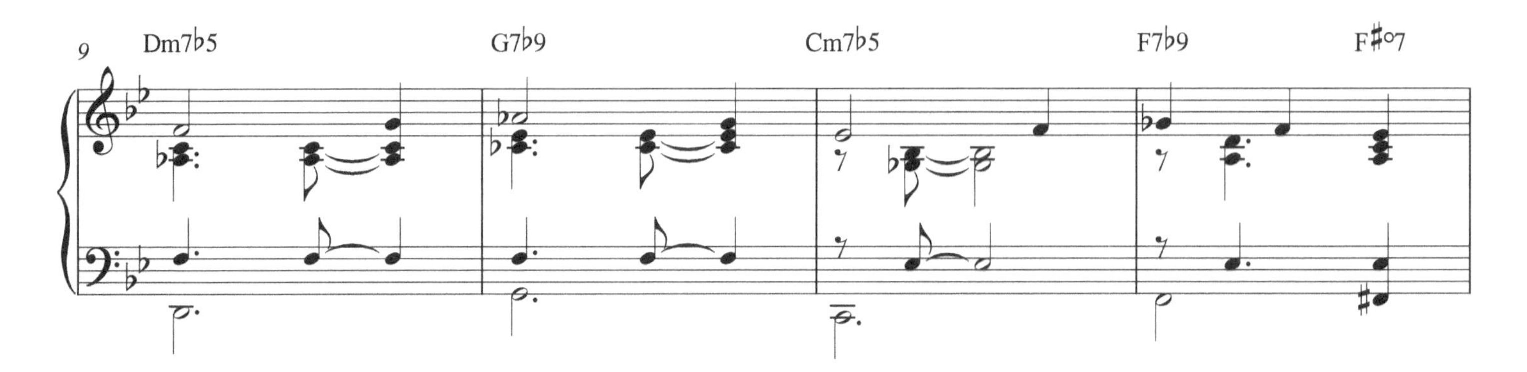
9
Dm7♭5
G7♭9
Cm7♭5
F7♭9
F♯o7

13
Gm7
C7
F7
C♭7

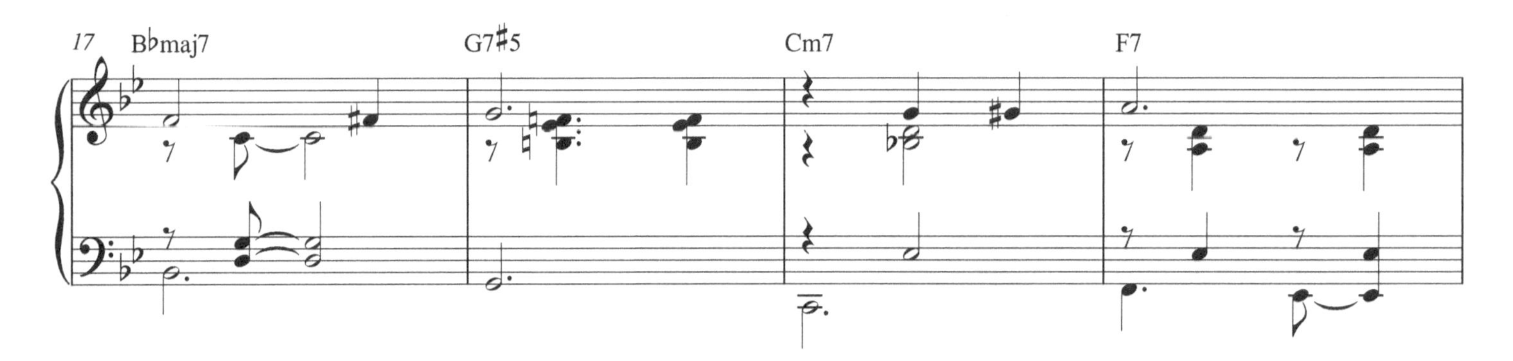
17
B♭maj7
G7♯5
Cm7
F7

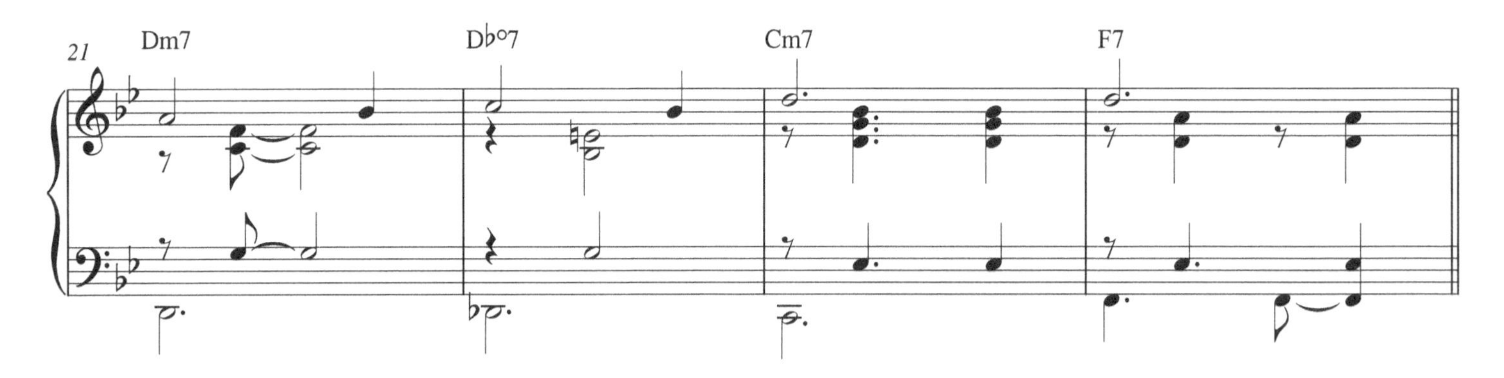
21
Dm7
D♭o7
Cm7
F7

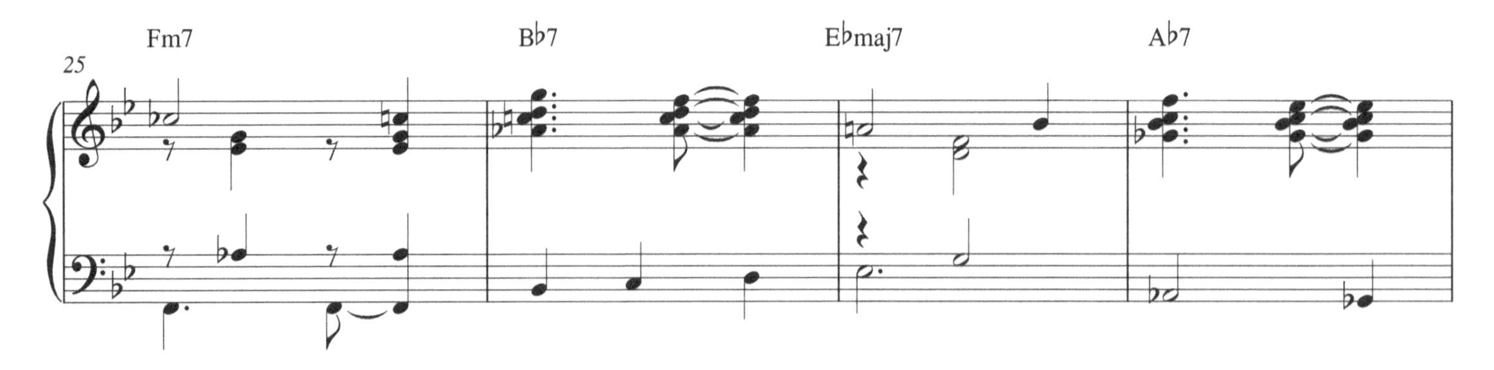
25
Fm7
B♭7
E♭maj7
A♭7

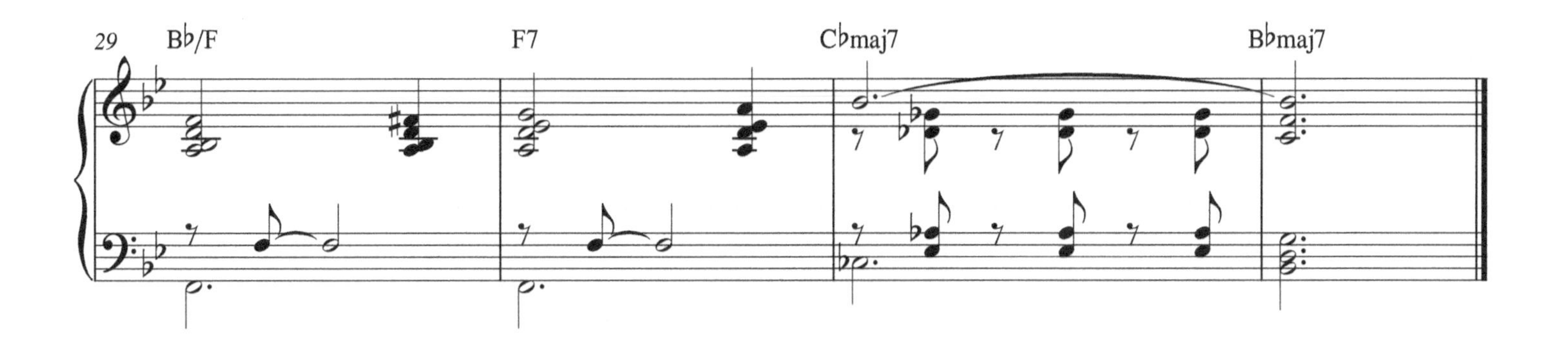

Suggested Jazz Waltzes to Play

Someday My Prince Will Come

Emily

Alice in Wonderland

The Boy Next Door

CHAPTER 7

LATIN JAZZ TUNES

Playing Latin tunes presents several issues for the solo pianist. One must keep a definitive Latin groove going while playing melody, chords, and bass. This is best accomplished by creating a composite Latin-tinged rhythm among all the parts. When the melody is most active, the accompanying chords can be less so and vice versa. Let the rhythm among all parts contribute to the overall feel of the music. To do this, we should have a groove firmly implanted in our ears to plug in and out of. A few common comping patterns for Bossa Nova grooves are given below. The techniques described in this chapter can be applied all Latin Jazz styles by adjusting the rhythms accordingly.

BOSSA NOVA

While Bossa Nova rhythms should be flexible and played in a random, inconsistent manner, it is best to set a regular pattern during an introduction to establish the feel; this places the feel firmly in the ears of the player and listener. A few intro-like patterns are shown below.

The clave is a rhythmic idea associated with Afro-Cuban Latin music. There is some debate as to whether the Brazilian clave is a meaningful concept. It differs from the Afro-Cuban clave in just one regard, but this difference gives Brazilian-based music like Bossa Nova a jazz-like feeling. The Brazilian clave can be played in two ways: the 3:2 or the 2:3 version.

Brazilian Clave

Bossa Nova accompaniment rhythms can be based on one of these claves, but they need not strictly adhere to them. The ideal Bossa accompaniment should be flexible and interdependent with the rhythms of the melody.

Bossa Nova Rhythmic Grooves

Some common Bossa Nova rhythmic patterns are shown below. The first is based on the 3:2 clave and the second is based on the 2:3 clave. There are many other possibilities. The bass parts consist of simple roots and fifths in a half-note rhythm.

Track 55

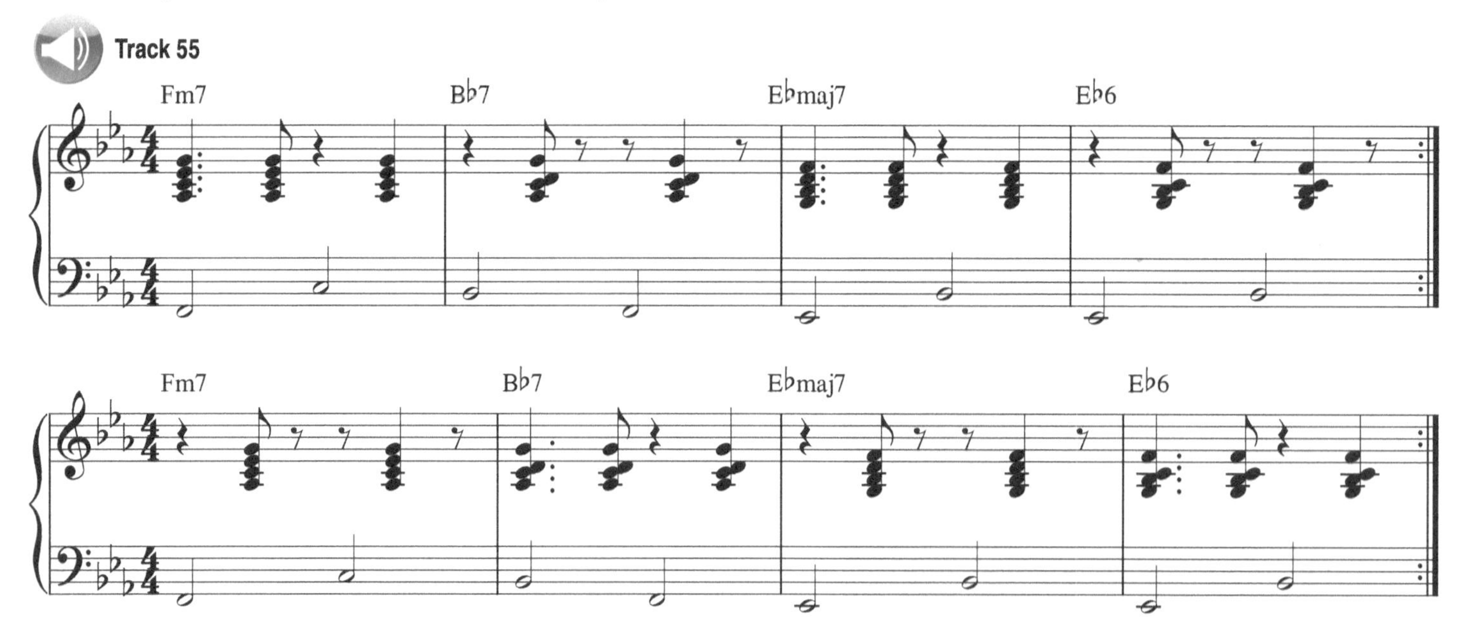

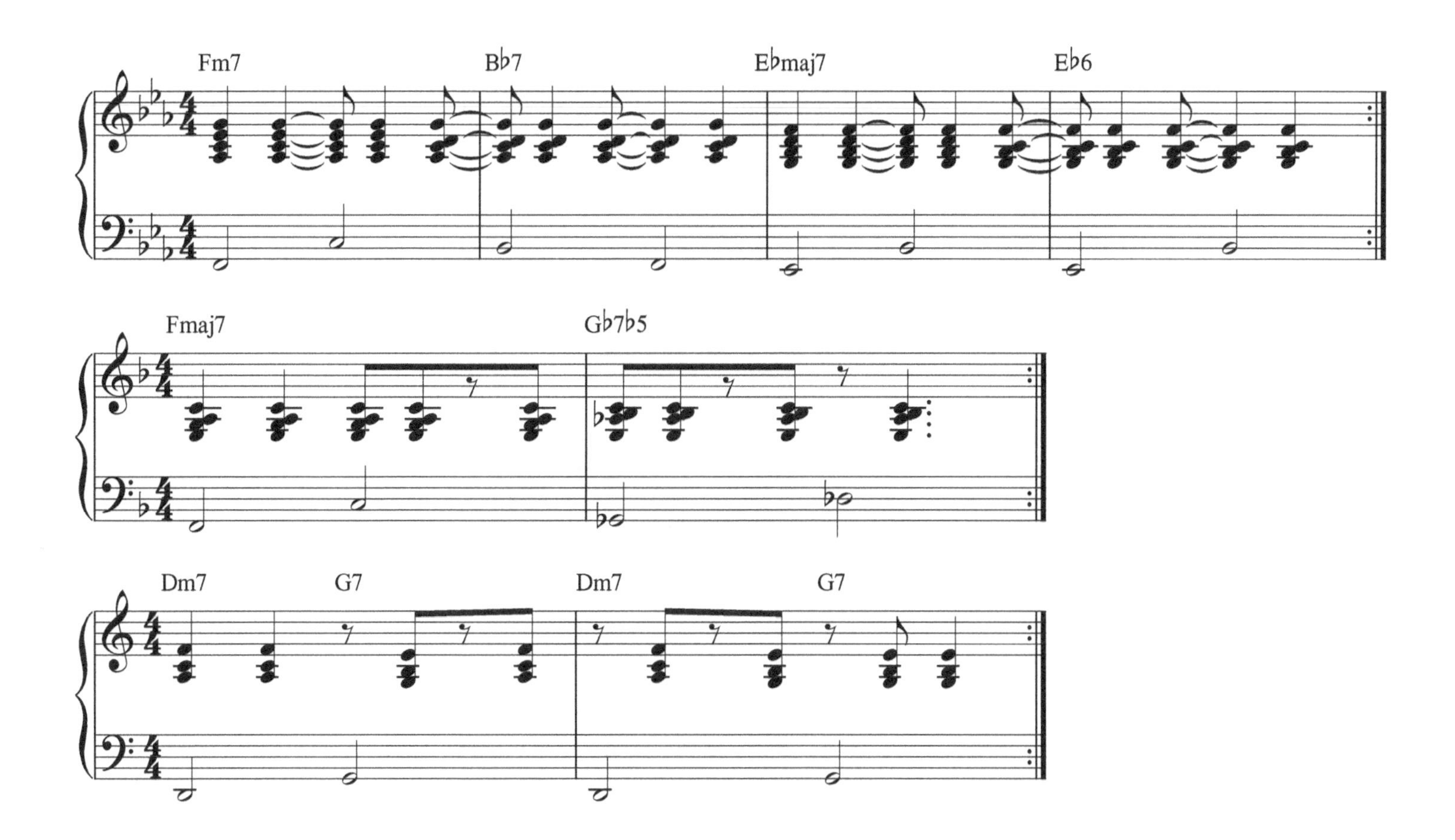

"VELA"

An convincing Latin Jazz performance should include a variety of accompaniment patterns, bass parts, and voicings. Suggestions for practicing a Bossa Nova are demonstrated below for "Vela."

Melody and Simple Bass

Play the melody with a simple half-note bass part of roots and fifths.

Track 56

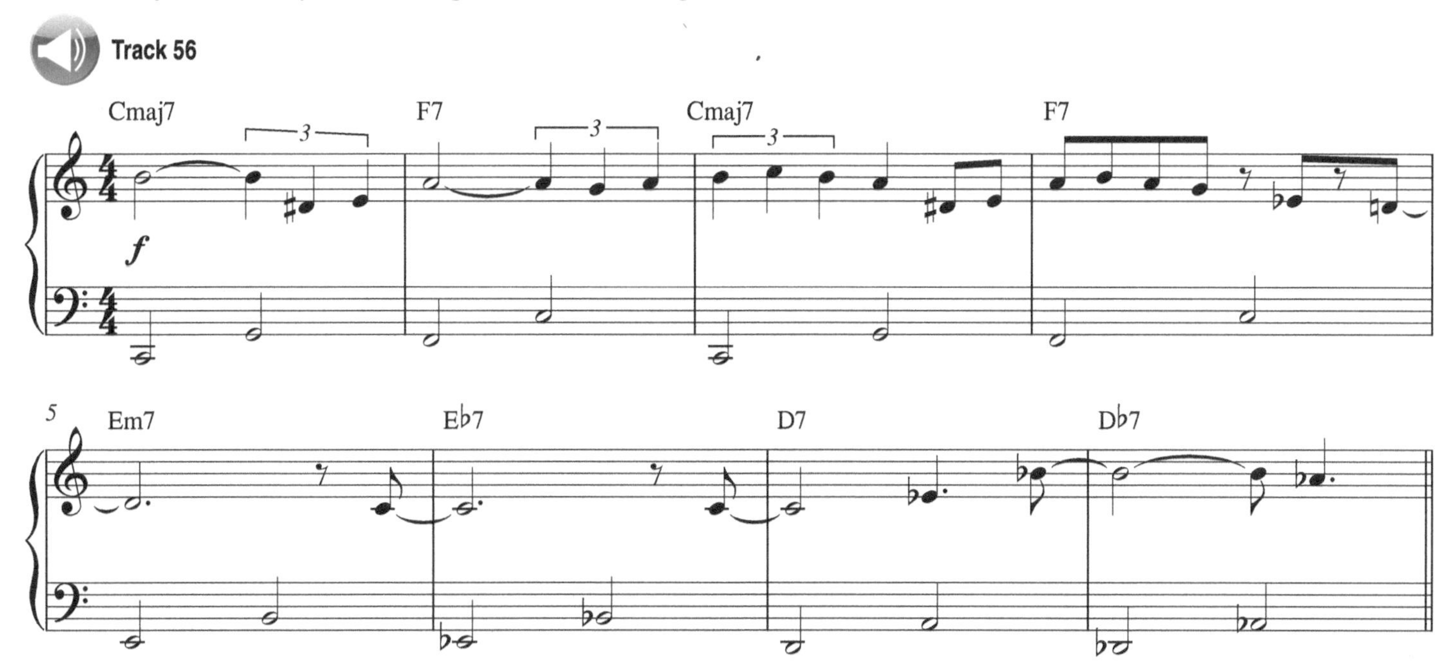

Melody and Harmonized Bass

The bass part can be amplified by playing a chord tone along with a bass note. Notice that this occurs only on the second bass note of the measure (beat 3), using the third and fifth or the third and seventh. This treatment provides the basic harmony while maintaining a consistent half-note bass pattern.

Track 57

Melody and Baion Bass

The bass can be made more rhythmically active by applying a basic baion rhythm. There are many variations on this rhythm; a few examples follow.

Track 58

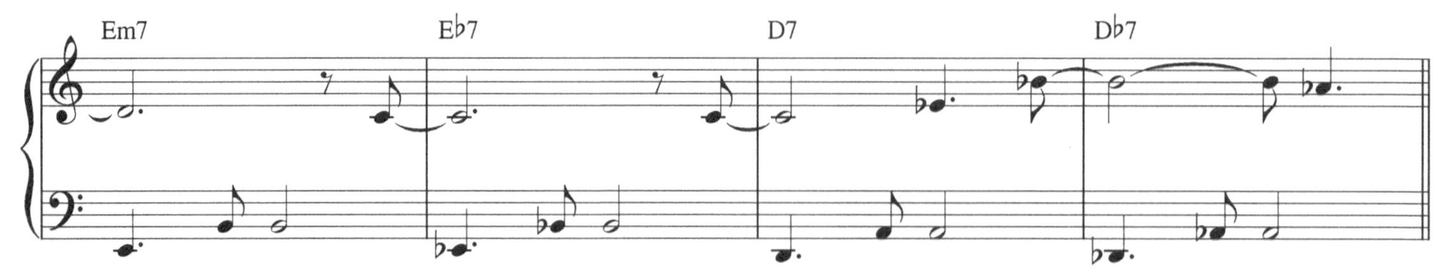

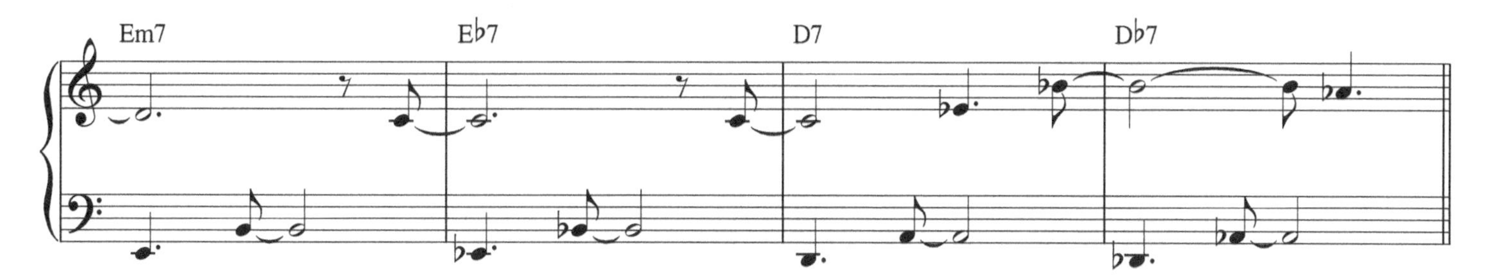

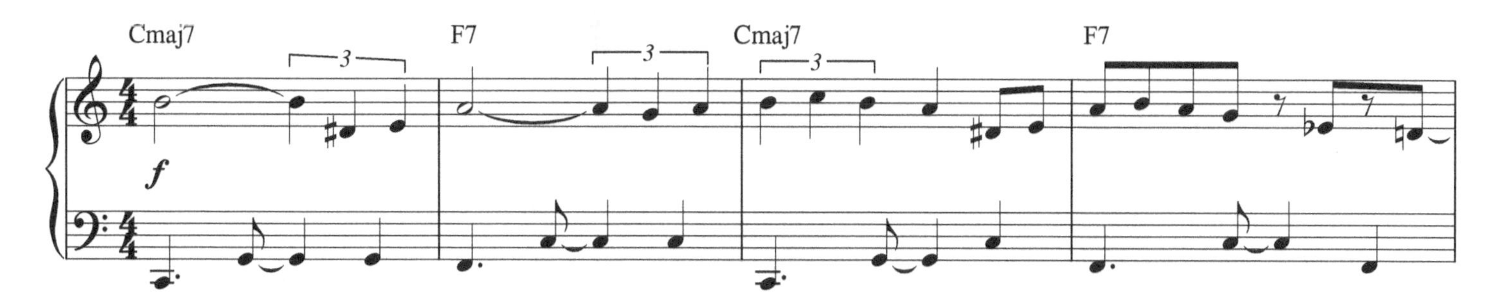

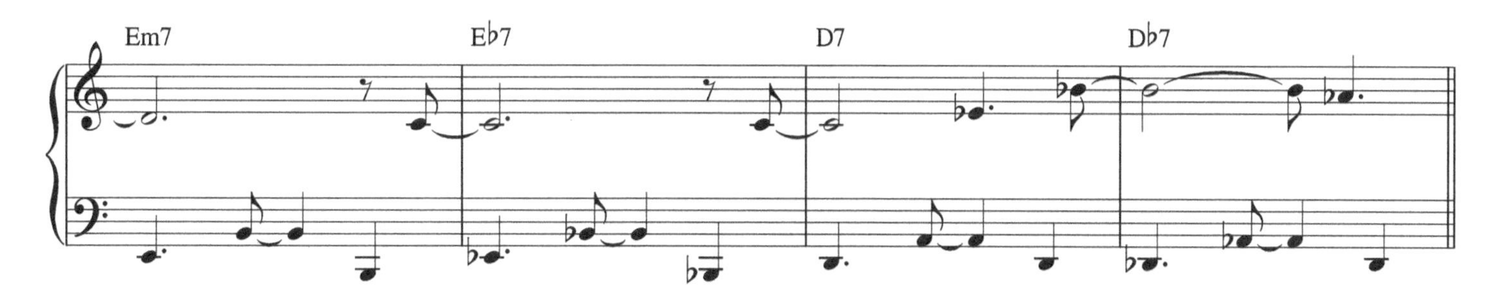

The baion bass rhythm can be played while outlining the harmony in the left hand.

Track 59

Right-Hand Comping with Left-Hand Bass

Play through the chord progression of "Vela" with Bossa Nova comping rhythms in the right hand and a simple bass part in the left hand. The following example demonstrates several ways to do this.

Track 60

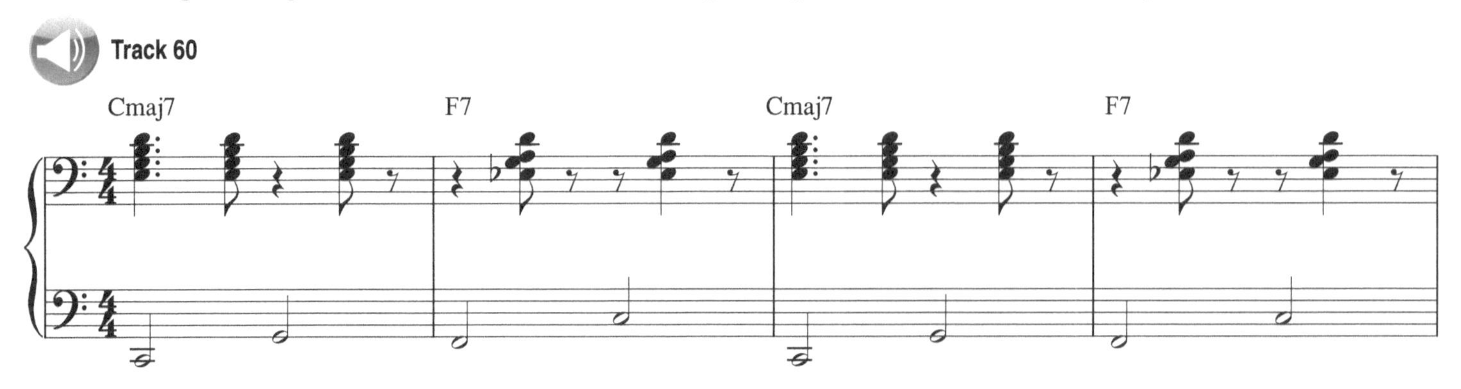

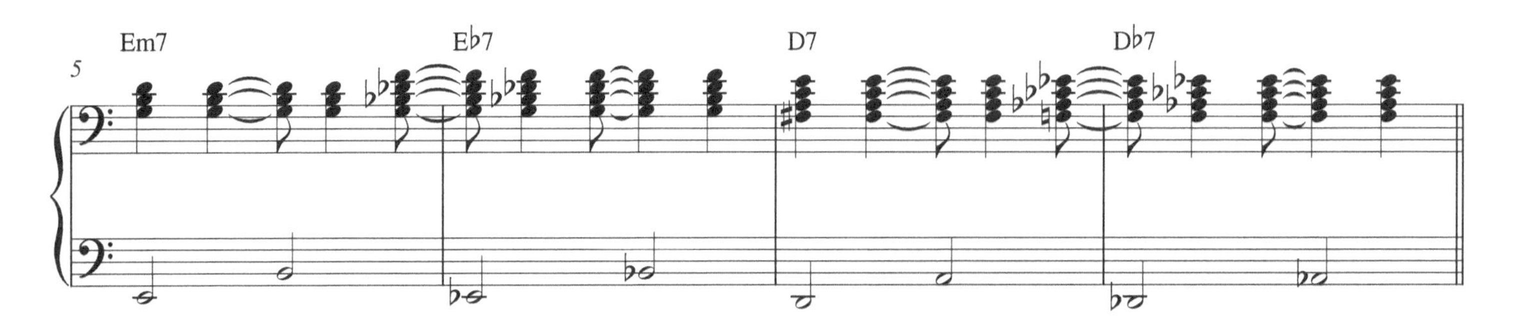

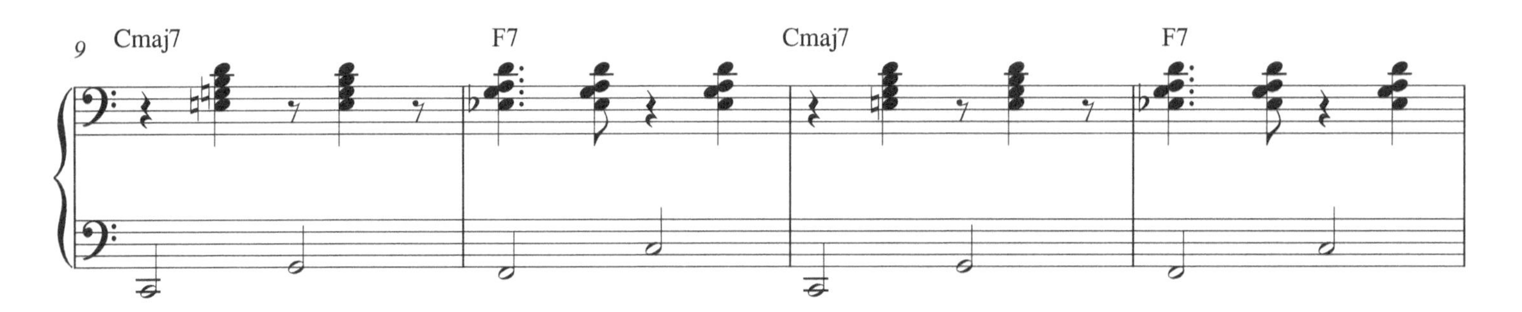

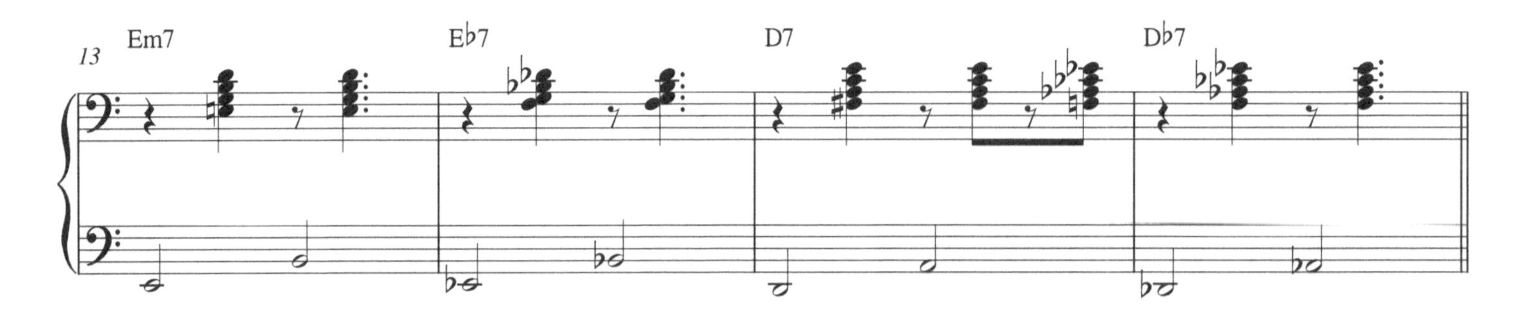

Right-Hand Melody and Chords with Left-Hand Bass

Track 61

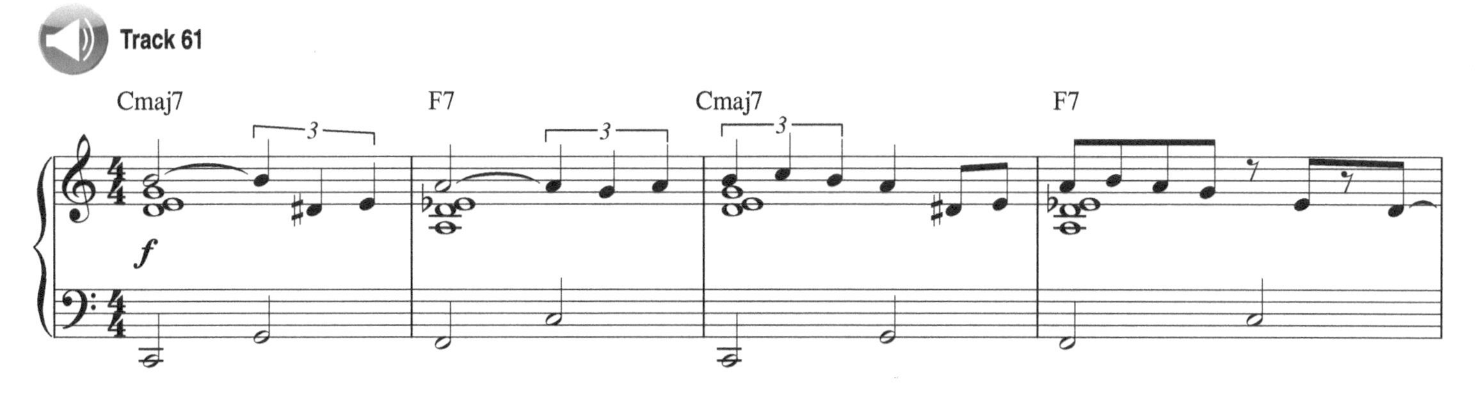

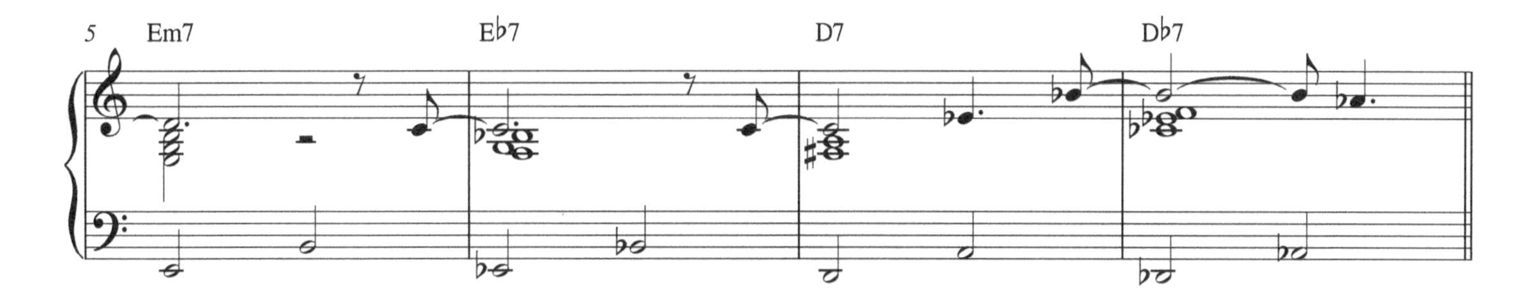

Right-Hand Melody and Comping

Playing melody and bass while comping chords in a Latin style can be a challenge, but the trick is to let the melody carry the rhythm and feel, along with the comping chords. Always think of the composite rhythm among the parts as implying the groove. One approach to "Vela" follows.

Track 62

Right-Hand Melody and Open Voicings in Both Hands

These voicing are chosen with comping in mind.

Track 63

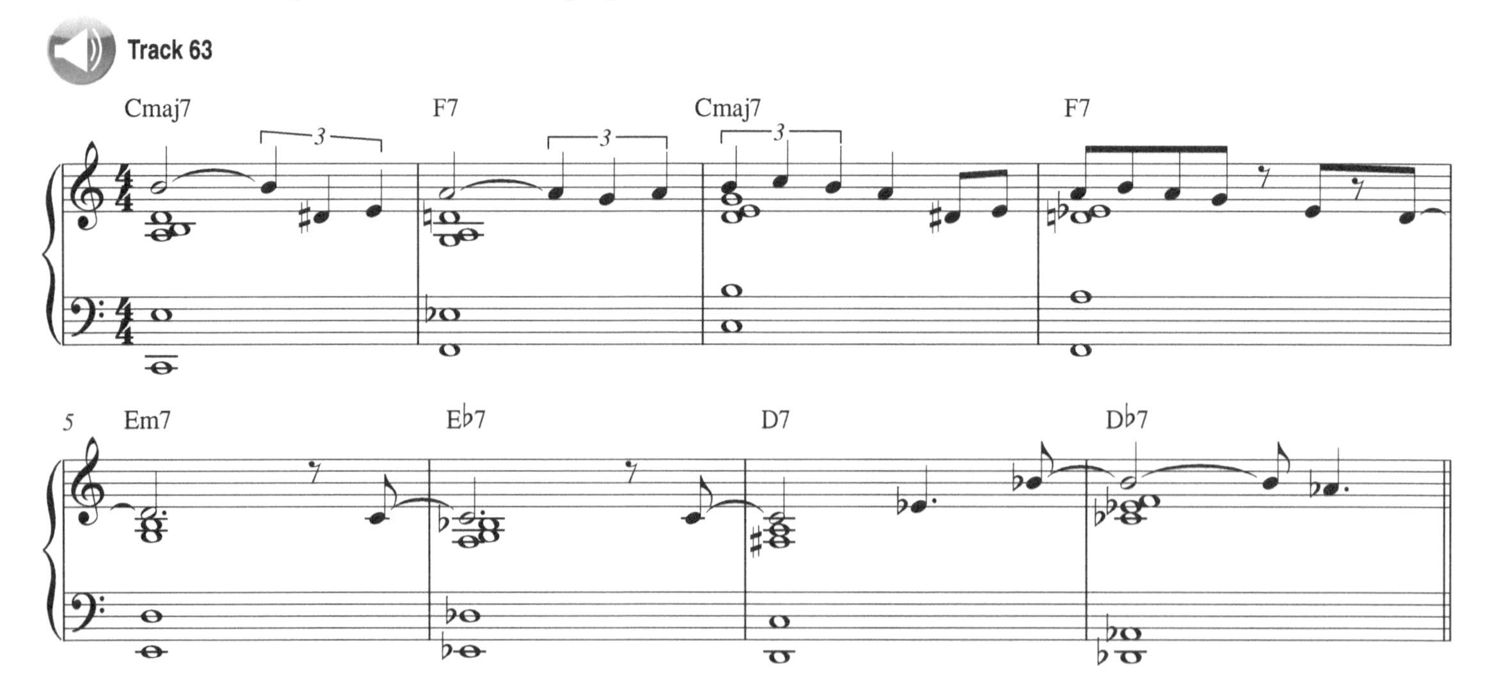

Right-Hand Melody with Open-Voicing Comping

In this example, the roots of the chord voicings are separated from the rest of the voicing. This allows for a richer texture without sacrificing much of the synergy among the three layers of melody, harmony, and bass.

Track 64

Melody with Staggered Open-Voicing Comping

This approach combines the open voicings with a half-note left-hand bass part by displacing the notes of the voicings from each other to create an active composite rhythm.

Track 65

Combined Solo Arrangement

This arrangement of "Vela" combines most of the techniques described above. Try your own arrangements and improvised versions.

Track 66

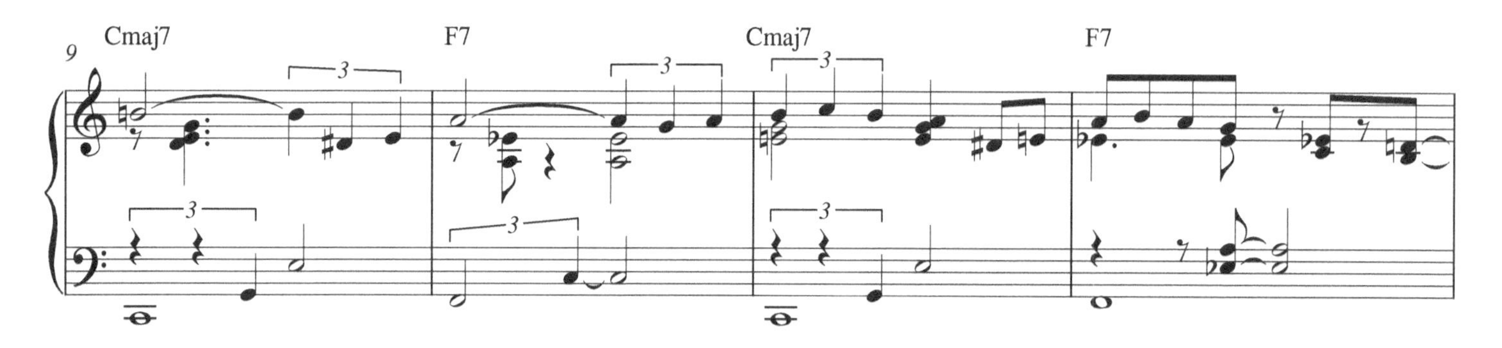

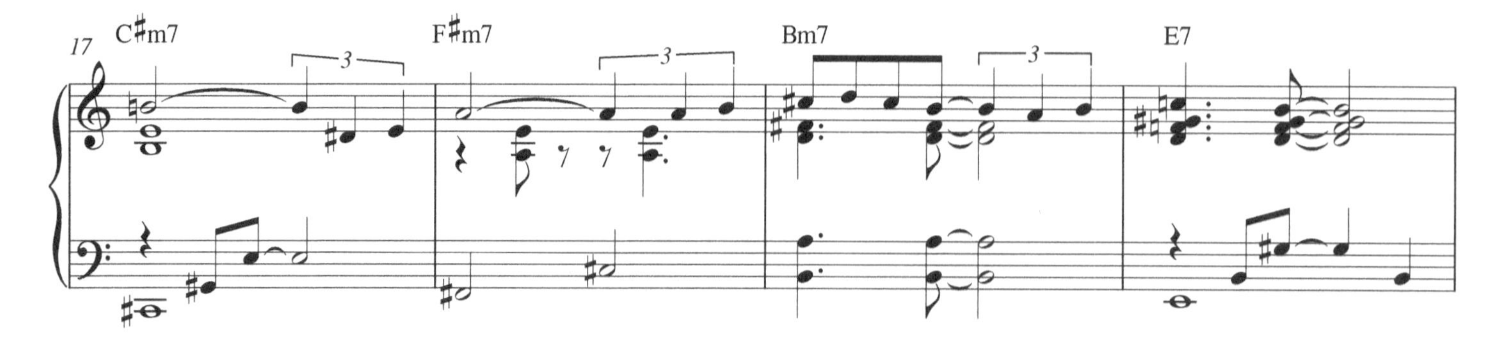

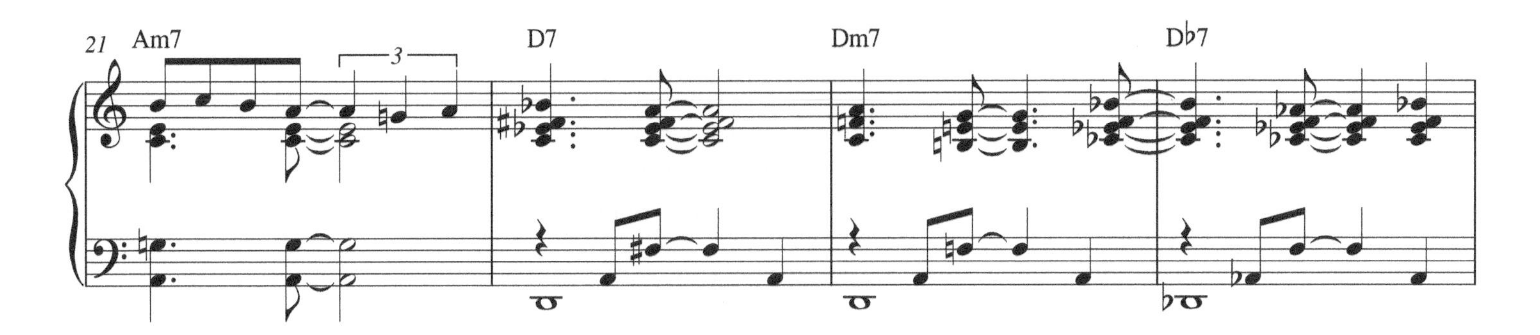

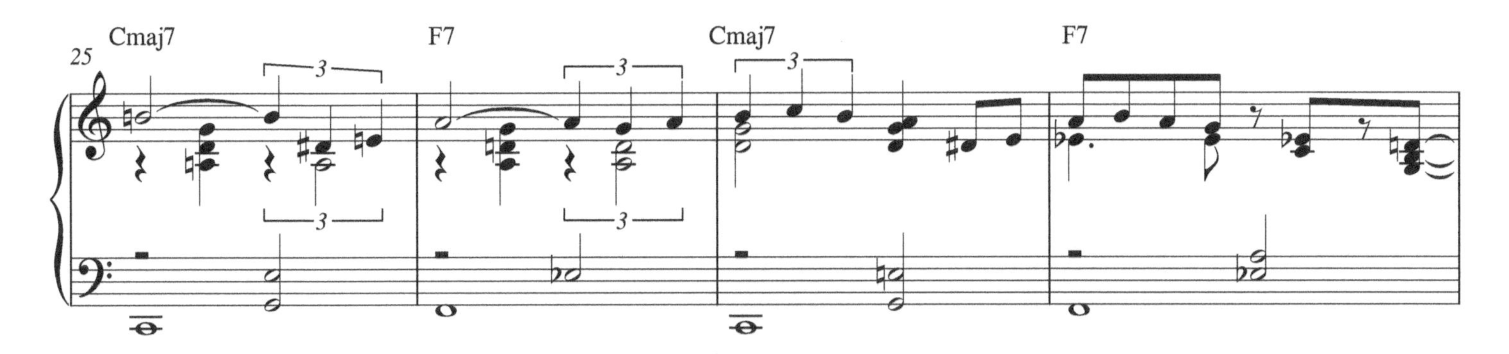

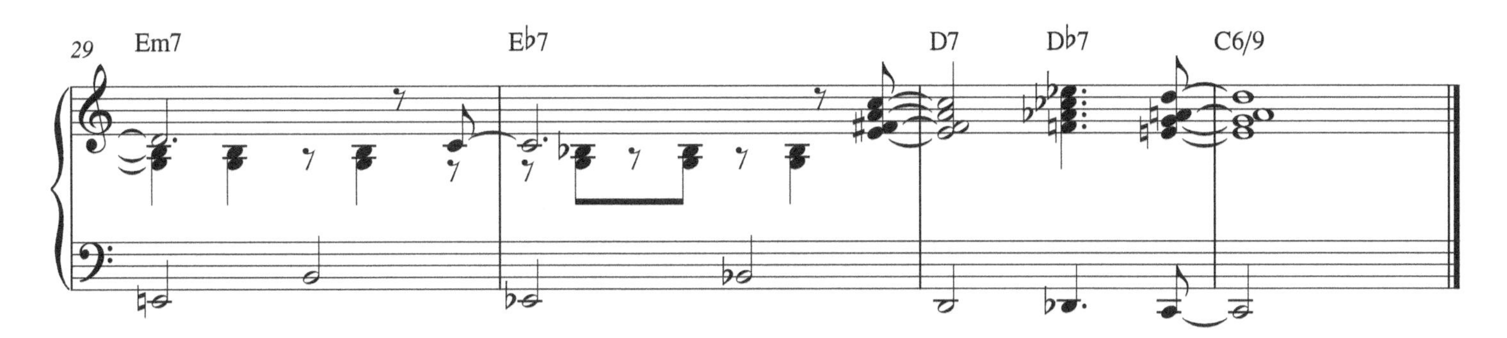

Suggested Bossa Novas to Play

Manha da Carnival (aka "Black Orpheus" and "The Day in the Life of a Fool")

Corcovado

The Girl from Ipanema

If You Never Come to Me

Gentle Rain

CHAPTER 8

BALLADS

Ballads offer the pianist more opportunities for harmonic elaboration and melodic embellishment. As with other styles, we need to familiarize ourselves with the melody, harmony, and bass of each tune. We'll use the old standard "My Melancholy Baby" as an example.

"MY MELANCHOLY BABY"

Melody and Bass

Play just the melody with a simple bass part.

Track 67

Melody and Simple Left-Hand Chords

Play simple left-hand chords with the right-hand melody.

Track 68

Right-Hand Melody and Chords with Left-Hand Bass

Play rootless chords below the right-hand melody while playing the simple bass in the left hand.

Track 69

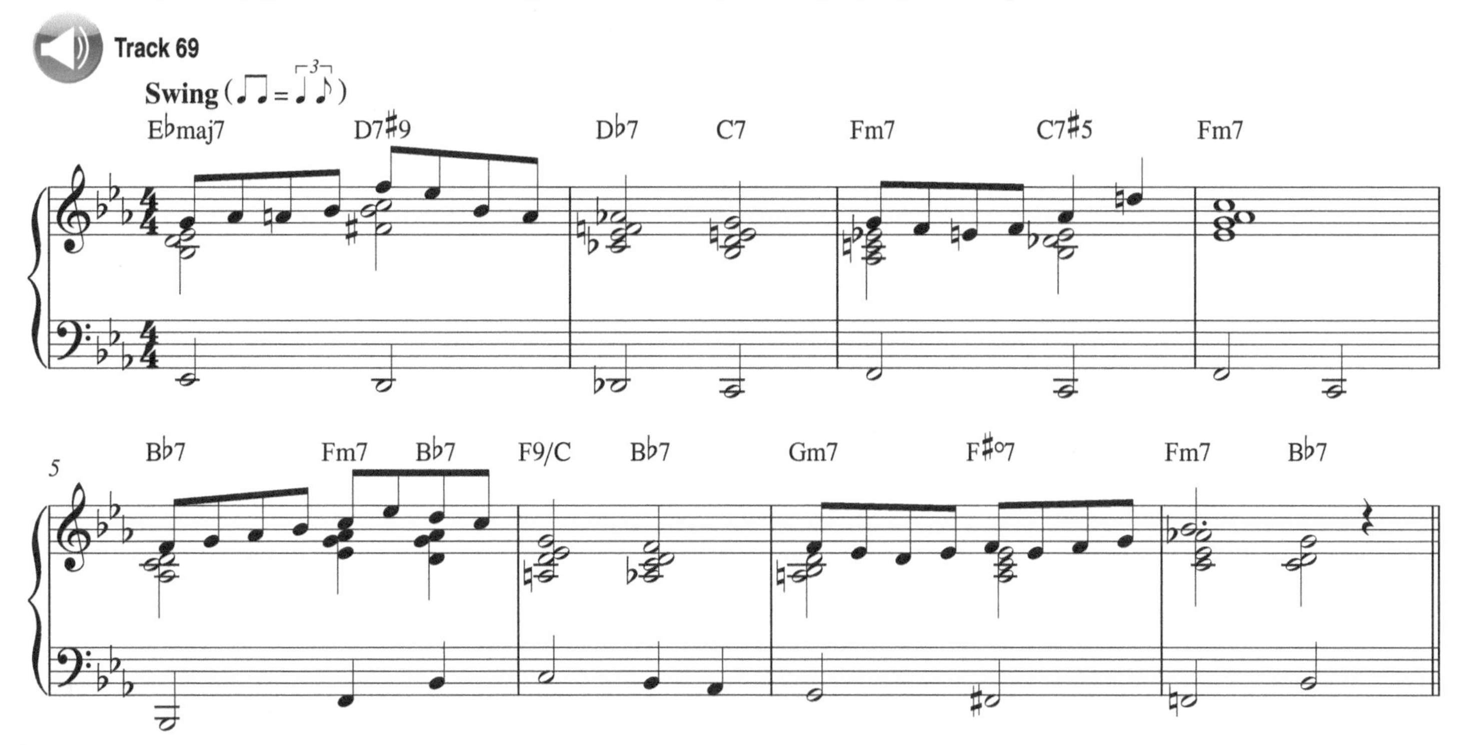

Melody with Open Voicings in Both Hands

Play full open voicings with both hands below the melody. The following example is one of many ways to do this.

Track 70

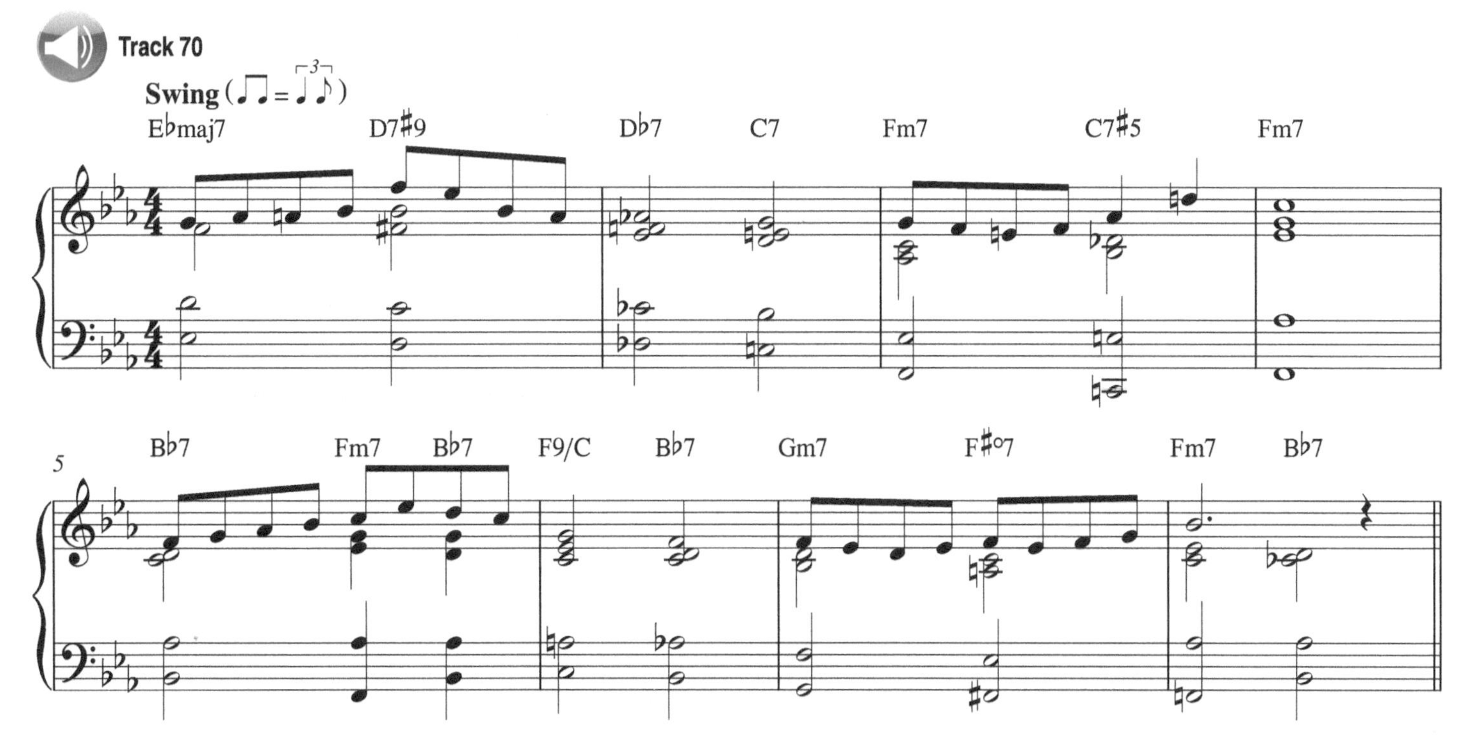

Combined Solo Arrangement

This arrangement of "My Melancholy Baby" combines several of the techniques used above and adds motion through staggered (displaced) voicings, re-harmonization, passing tones, and moving lines.

Track 71

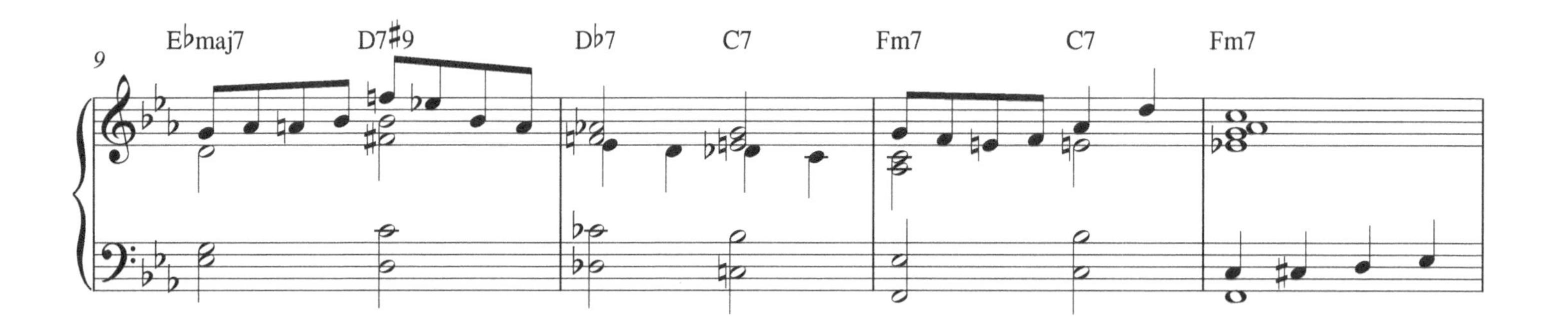

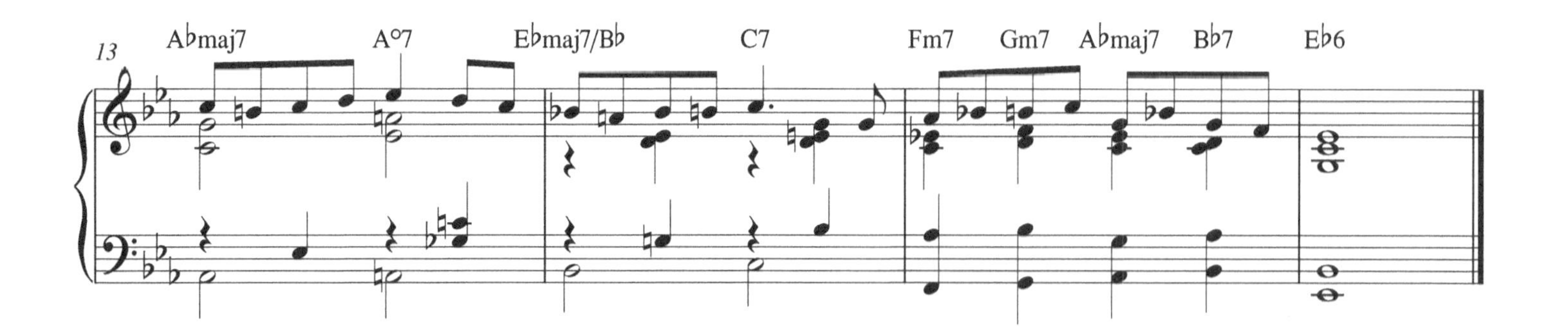

Melody with Left-Hand Rootless Voicings

Play rootless voicings in the left-hand with the right-hand melody.

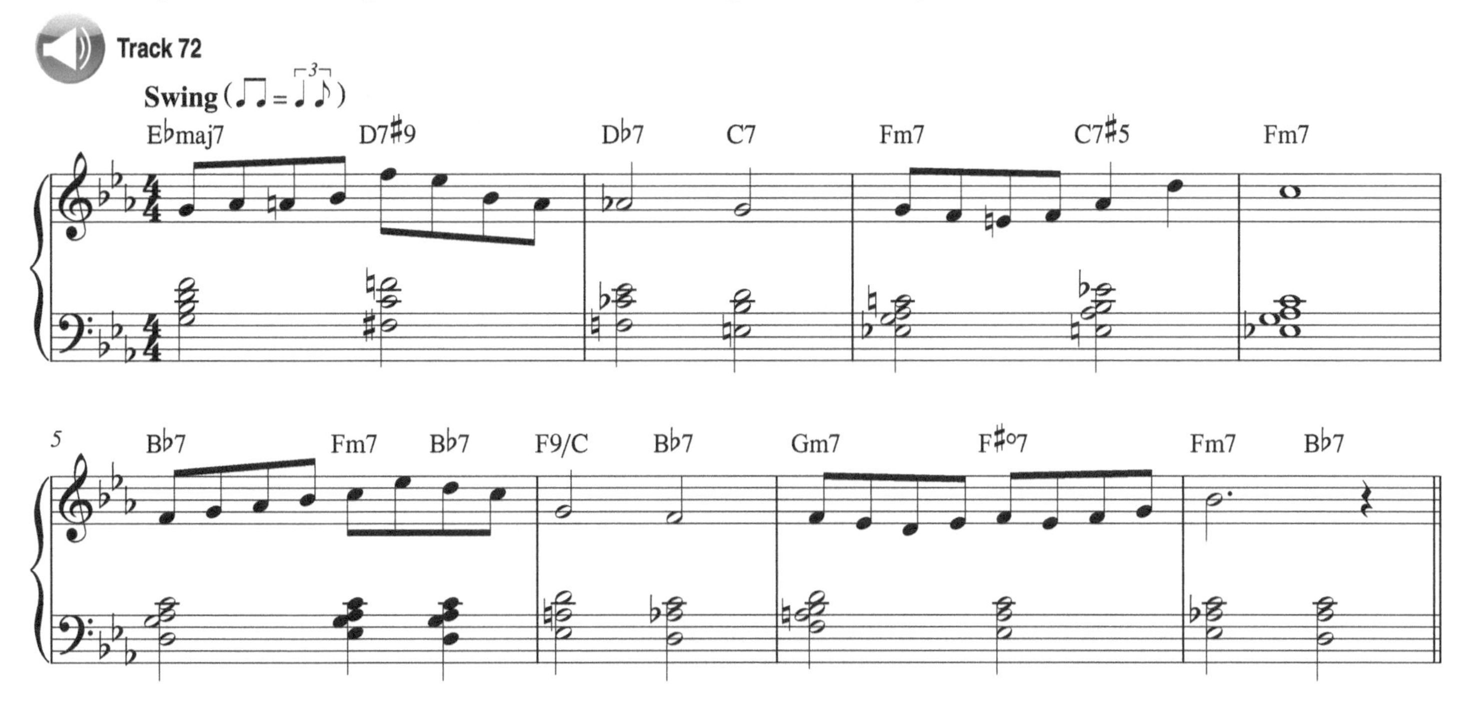

Melody with Striding Left Hand

Striding the left hand from bass notes to rootless chords can be used effectively for ballads. One of many possibilities follows.

Rubato Treatment

Ballads are often played either wholly or partly in a rubato or tempo ad lib manner. Avoiding strict time allows you to embellish and decorate the written melody and harmony in inventive and virtuosic ways. Left-hand arpeggios are regularly used in rubato playing.

Track 74

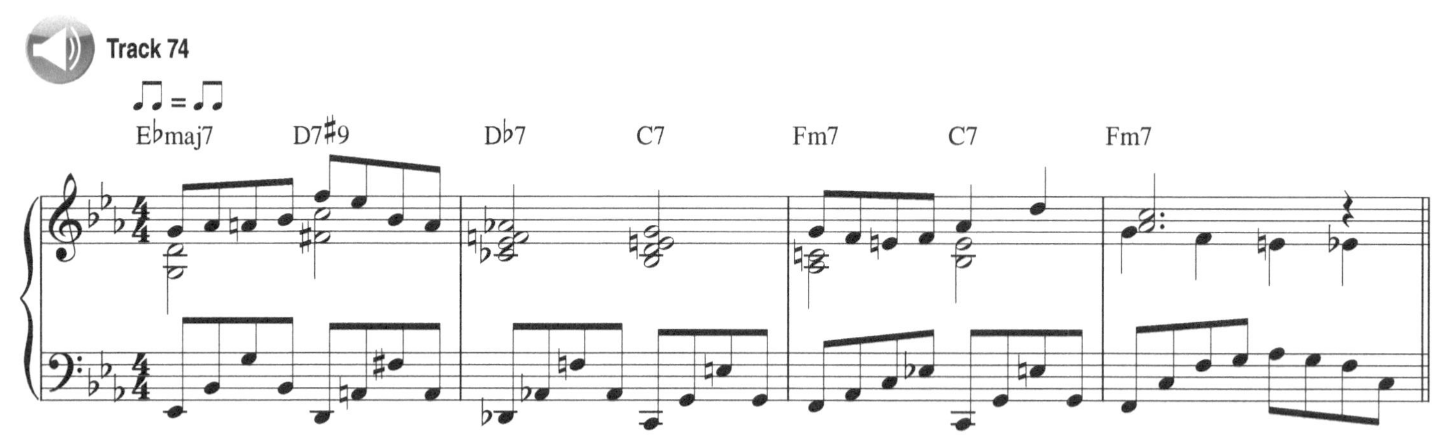

Here is an example of a rubato approach to "My Melancholy Baby," with re-harmonizations and an active left hand. Play with a flexible beat and generous use of the pedal. This type of playing can be used for introductions to any kind of tune.

Track 75

Freely, molto rubato

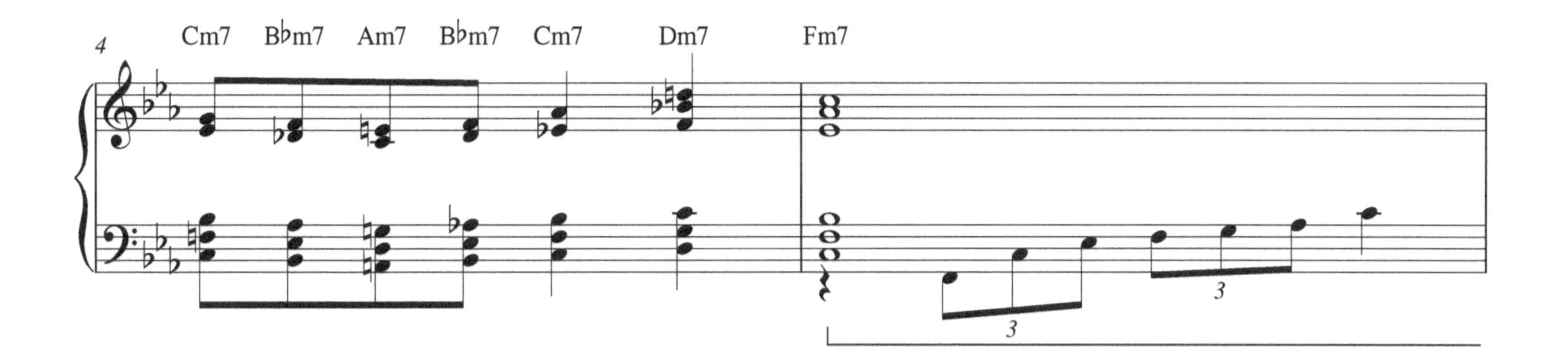
4
Cm7
B♭m7
Am7
B♭m7
Cm7
Dm7
Fm7
3
3

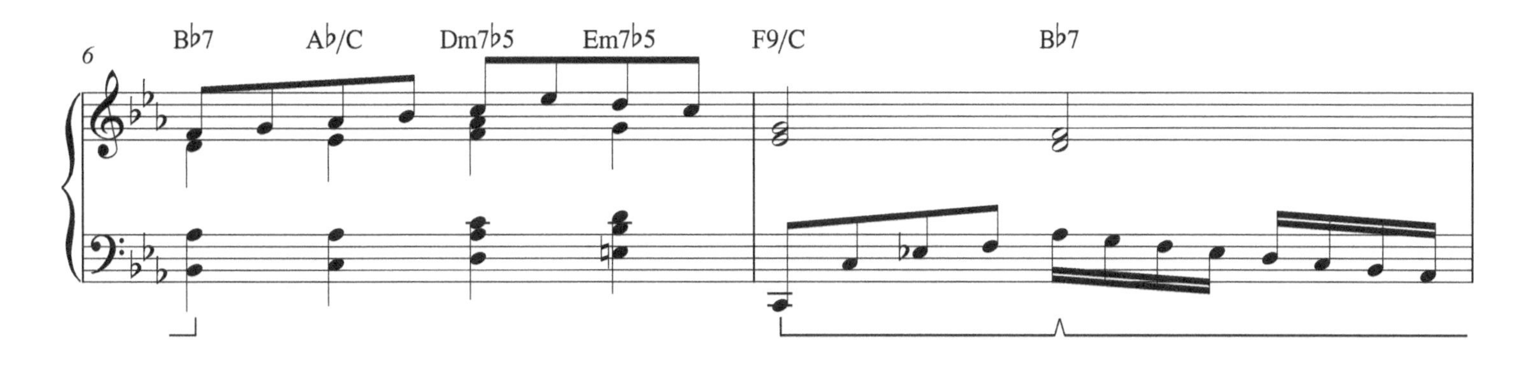
6
B♭7
A♭/C
Dm7♭5
Em7♭5
F9/C
B♭7

8
Gm7
F♯°7
Fm11
A♭m9
B♭7♭9

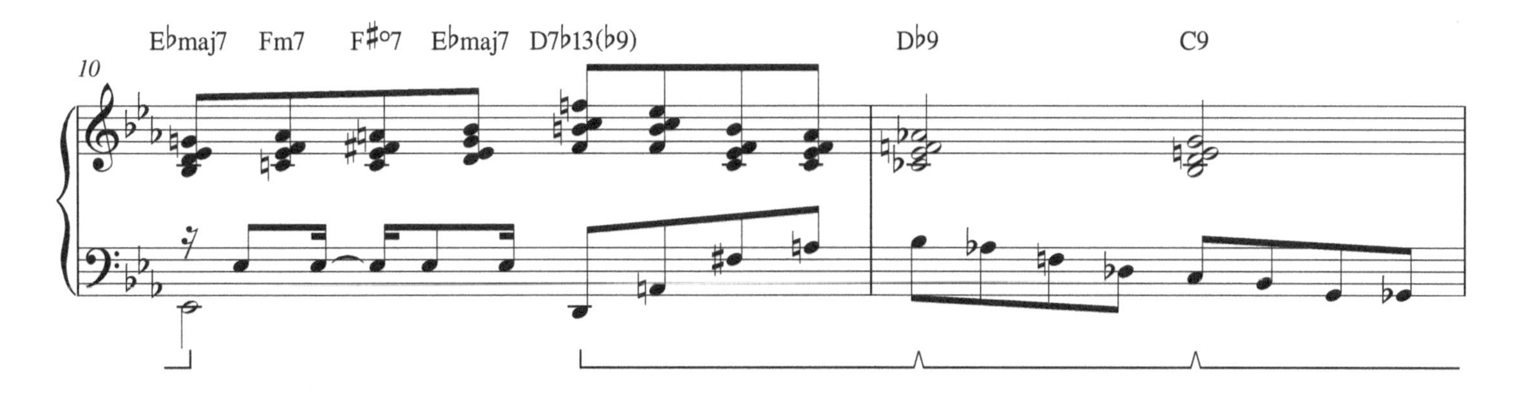
10
E♭maj7
Fm7
F♯°7
E♭maj7
D7♭13(♭9)
D♭9
C9

12
Fm7
C9
Fm7

Suggested Ballads to Play

Body and Soul

Lover Man

In a Sentimental Mood

I Fall in Love Too Easily

CHAPTER 9
IMPROVISATION

Improvisation presents many challenges for the solo jazz pianist. The difference between playing tunes and improvising on those tunes is a mental one. We know how the tune goes, even if we change it as it is played; we don't know how the improvisation will go and must make split-second decisions as the music unfolds. So far, the solo piano techniques used in this book have applied to the playing of tunes. While all these techniques are used during improvisations, a simpler approach is often necessary when the improvised lines are most active. In other words, keeping with the composite rhythm approach of this book, less is more when accompanying an active melody. A few samples of improvisations on a few tunes used in the book follow. Let the right hand carry the rhythmic impulse along with your left hand, rather than relying on your left hand alone to keep the pulse going.

The same steps used to decipher tunes can be used to practice solo improvisation – including playing with half-note and quarter-note bass lines, simple left-hand chords, guide tones, combined techniques, etc.

"Winter Comes"

Below is an improvisation on the first part of "Winter Comes," with a bass line in a "two" feel.

"Rose Room"

The next example is an improvisation on the first part of "Rose Room," with a walking bass line and a chord melody.

"Indiana"

This improvisation on "Indiana" makes use of a boppish single-note melodic line in the right hand throughout. The left hand complements the right hand with a mixture of shell voicings, guide tone voicings, and bass notes.

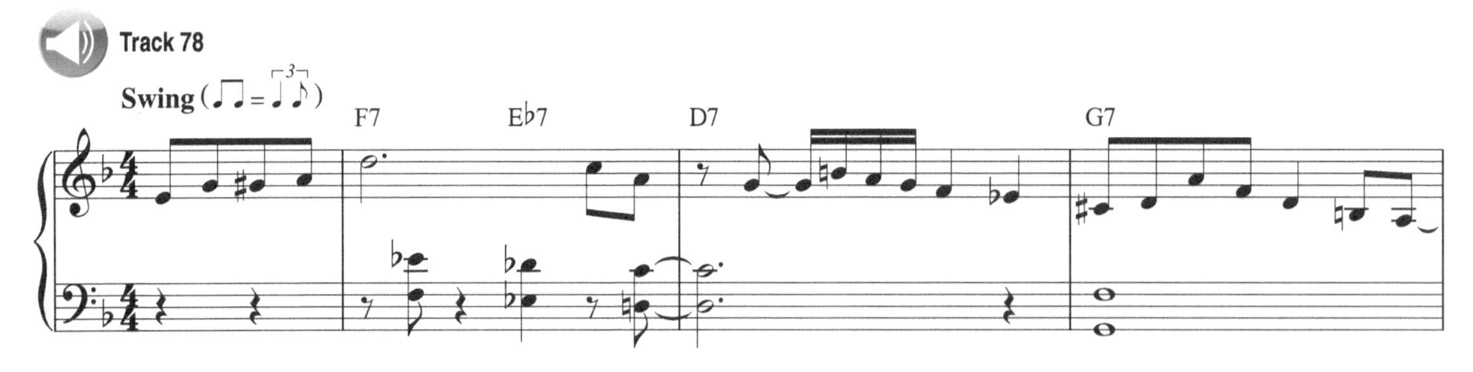

8
Cm7
B7
B♭maj7
E♭7
Fmaj7
E♭7

12
D7
G7
C7

16
G♭7
F
E♭7
D7
G7

21
Em7
3
A7
3
Dm7
D♭7

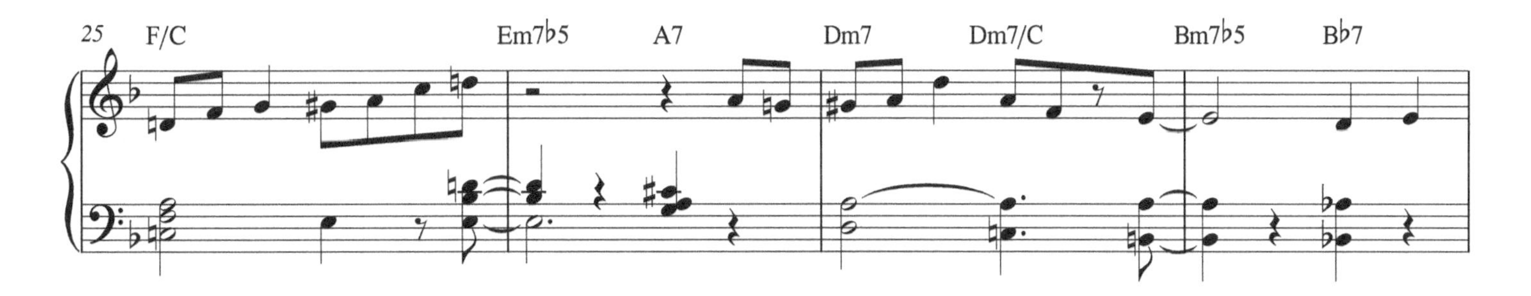
25
F/C
Em7♭5
A7
Dm7
Dm7/C
Bm7♭5
B♭7

29
Am7
D7
Gm7
G♭7
F6
Gm7
G♭7

"Wendy's Waltz"

In this excerpt from the beginning of "Wendy's Waltz" the left hand keeps a jazz waltz feel going simply with a light texture. Meanwhile, the right hand roams through the chord changes.

Track 79

"Vela"

In this improvisation on the first part of "Vela," the left hand sets a simple groove with bass and chord tones. The right hand plays a single-note melody, with occasional chords that fill the spaces left by the held notes.

Track 80

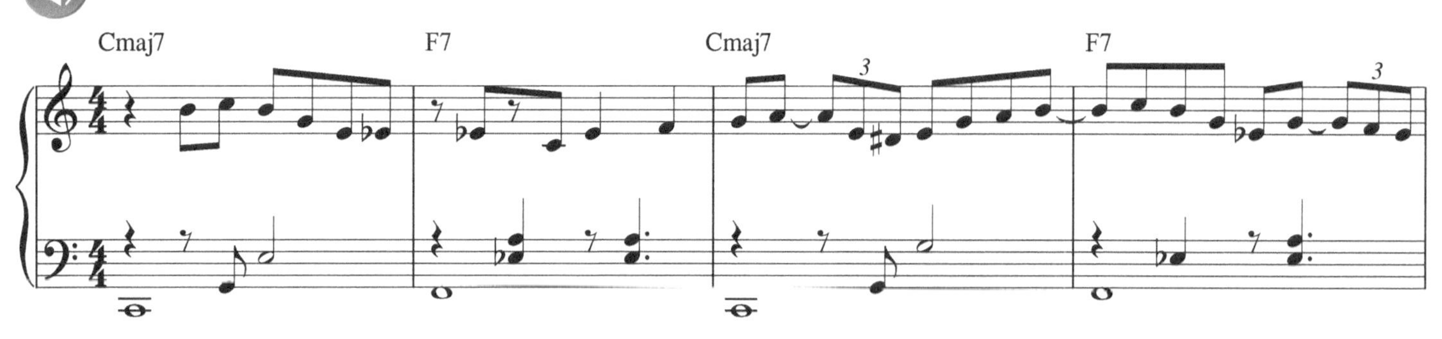

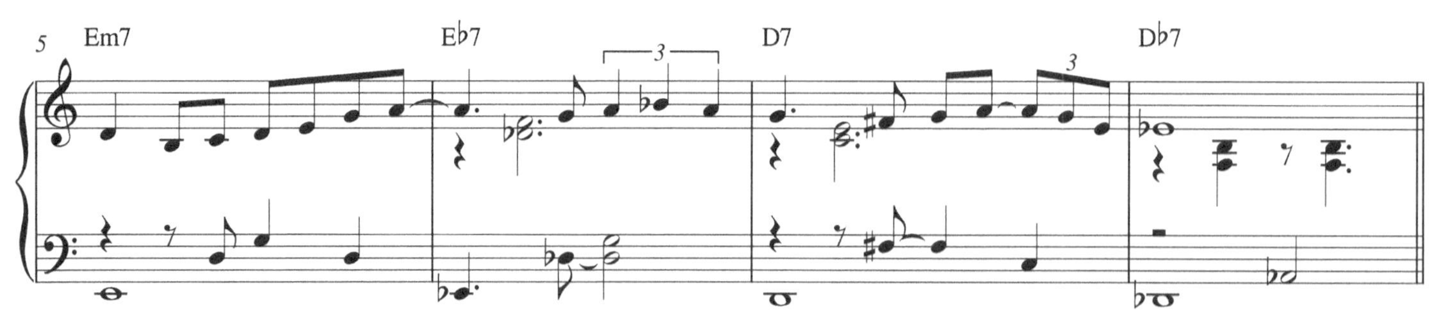

"My Melancholy Baby"

For this improvisation on the first half of "My Melancholy Baby," the left hand combines elements of stride with simple chording and bass movement. For the most part, the right hand plays a decorative melody with one chord on the longest-held note.

Track 81

LEAD SHEETS

Indiana
(Back Home Again in Indiana)

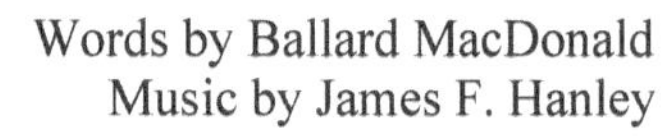

9
Ebmaj7 D7#9 Db7 C7 Fm7 C7 Fm7
13
Abmaj7 Adim7 Ebmaj7/Bb C7 Fm7 Bb7 Eb6
Copyright © 2016 by HAL LEONARD CORPORATION
International Copyright Secured All Rights Reserved
Poor Butterfly
Words by John L. Golden
Music by Raymond Hubbel
Medium Swing
Bbm7 Eb7sus Eb7b9 Abdim7 Abmaj7
5
C+7#9 F7 Cm7 F7
9
Bbm7 Eb7 Gm7b5 C7b9 Fm7
13
Bb7 Eb7sus Eb7
17
Bbm7 Eb7sus Eb7b9 Abdim7 Abmaj7
21
C+7#9 F7 Cm7 F7
25
Bbm7 Dbm7 Gb7 Cm7 Db7 Cm7 Bdim7
29
Bbm7 Eb7 Abdim7 Abmaj7
Copyright © 2016 by HAL LEONARD CORPORATION
International Copyright Secured All Rights Reserved

Rose Room

Words by Harry Williams
Music by Art Hickman

St. Louis Blues

Words and Music by
W.C. Handy

Wendy's Waltz

By John Valerio

When You and I Were Young, Maggie

Words by George W. Johnson
Music by James Austin Butterfield

Winter Comes

By John Valerio

ABOUT THE AUTHOR

Philadelphia native John Valerio is a pianist, composer, and author. He holds a doctorate in composition from Temple University and has written numerous works for a variety of voices, instruments, and ensembles – in both classical and jazz idioms. A versatile performer, Dr. Valerio has worked with many outstanding jazz artists, in concerts and in clubs. For Hal Leonard Corporation, he has published several internationally selling books on jazz piano, including *Bebop Jazz Piano* and *Jazz Piano Technique*. Dr. Valerio is on the faculty of the University of South Carolina, in addition to giving private piano instruction.

jazz piano solos series

INCLUDES CHORD NAMES!

Each volume features exciting new arrangements with chord symbols of the songs which helped define a style.

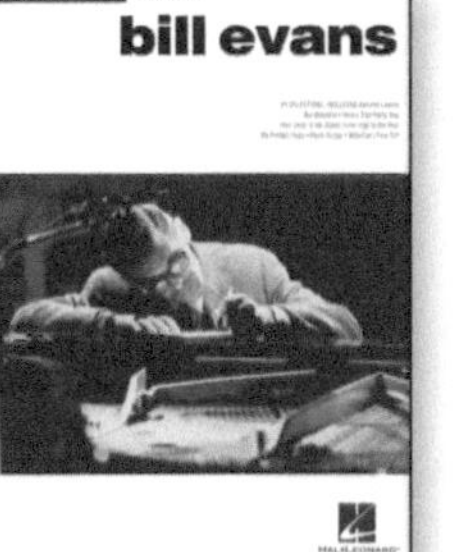

vol. 1 miles davis
00306521 .... $19.99

vol. 2 jazz blues
00306522 .... $17.99

vol. 3 latin jazz
00310621 .... $16.99

vol. 4 bebop jazz
00310709 .... $16.99

vol. 5 cool jazz
00310710 .... $16.99

vol. 6 hard bop
00323507 .... $16.99

vol. 7 smooth jazz
00310727 .... $16.99

vol. 8 jazz pop
00311786 .... $17.99

vol. 9 duke ellington
00311787 .... $17.99

vol. 10 jazz ballads
00311788 .... $17.99

vol. 11 soul jazz
00311789 .... $17.99

vol. 12 swinging jazz
00311797 .... $17.99

vol. 13 jazz gems
00311899 .... $16.99

vol. 14 jazz classics
00311900 .... $16.99

vol. 15 bossa nova
00311906 .... $17.99

vol. 16 disney
00312121 .... $17.99

vol. 17 antonio carlos jobim
00312122 .... $17.99

vol. 18 modern jazz quartet
00307270 .... $16.99

vol. 19 bill evans
00307273 .... $19.99

vol. 20 gypsy jazz
00307289 .... $16.99

vol. 21 new orleans
00312169 .... $16.99

vol. 22 classic jazz
00001529 .... $17.99

vol. 23 jazz for lovers
00312548 .... $16.99

vol. 24 john coltrane
00307395 .... $17.99

vol. 25 christmas songs
00101790 .... $17.99

vol. 26 george gershwin
00103353 .... $17.99

vol. 27 late night jazz
00312547 .... $17.99

vol. 28 the beatles
00119302 .... $19.99

vol. 29 elton john
00120968 .... $19.99

vol. 30 cole porter
00123364 .... $17.99

vol. 31 cocktail piano
00123366 .... $17.99

vol. 32 johnny mercer
00123367 .... $16.99

vol. 33 gospel
00127079 .... $17.99

vol. 34 horace silver
00139633 .... $16.99

vol. 35 stride piano
00139685 .... $17.99

vol. 36 broadway jazz
00144365 .... $17.99

vol. 37 silver screen jazz
00144366 .... $16.99

vol. 38 henry mancini
00146382 .... $16.99

vol. 39 sacred christmas carols
00147678 .... $17.99

vol. 40 charlie parker
00149089 .... $16.99

vol. 41 pop standards
00153656 .... $16.99

vol. 42 dave brubeck
00154634 .... $16.99

vol. 43 candlelight jazz
00154901 .... $17.99

vol. 44 jazz standards
00160856 .... $17.99

vol. 45 christmas standards
00172024 .... $17.99

vol. 46 cocktail jazz
00172025 .... $17.99

vol. 47 hymns
00172026 .... $17.99

vol. 48 blue skies & other irving berlin songs
00197873 .... $16.99

vol. 49 thelonious monk
00232767 .... $16.99

vol. 50 best smooth jazz
00233277 .... $16.99

vol. 51 disney favorites
00233315 .... $16.99

vol. 52 bebop classics
00234075 .... $16.99

vol. 53 jazz-rock
00256715 .... $16.99

vol. 54 jazz fusion
00256716 .... $16.99

vol. 55 ragtime
00274961 .... $16.99

vol. 56 pop ballads
00274962 .... $16.99

vol. 57 pat metheny
00277058 .... $17.99

vol. 58 big band era
00284837 .... $17.99

vol. 59 west coast jazz
00290792 .... $17.99

vol. 60 boogie woogie
00363280 .... $17.99

vol. 61 christmas classics
00367872 .... $17.99

HAL•LEONARD®

View songlists and order online from your favorite music retailer at
www.halleonard.com

0621

Prices, contents & availability subject to change without notice. 427